C000151800

SAVED FROM THE WAVES

SAVED FROM THE WAVES

ANIMAL RESCUES OF THE RNLI

Lifeboats

with Nikki Croft-Girvan

HarperCollins*Publishers*

HarperCollins*Publishers*
1 London Bridge Street
London SE1 9GF

www.harpercollins.co.uk

HarperCollins*Publishers*
1st Floor, Watermarque Building, Ringsend Road
Dublin 4, Ireland

First published by HarperCollins*Publishers* 2022

1 3 5 7 9 10 8 6 4 2

A catalogue record of this book is
available from the British Library

ISBN 978-0-00-848596-2

Printed and bound in the UK using 100%
renewable electricity at CPI Group (UK) Ltd

MIX
Paper from
responsible sources
FSC™ C007454

This book is produced from independently certified FSC™ paper
to ensure responsible forest management.

For more information visit: www.harpercollins.co.uk/green

This book is dedicated to the animals
loved, lost and rescued – and the people
who have cared for them.

A minimum of £8,000 from the sale of this book will be paid in support of the RNLI. Payments are made to RNLI (Sales) Ltd, which pays all its taxable profits to the RNLI, a charity registered in England and Wales (209603), Scotland (SC037736), the Republic of Ireland (20003326), the Bailiwick of Jersey (14), the Isle of Man (1308 and 006329F) and the Bailiwick of Guernsey and Alderney, of West Quay Road, Poole, Dorset BN15 1HZ.

CONTENTS

FOREWORD

by Steve Backshall

I have always been grateful to the RNLI. My career as a wildlife broadcaster and my passion for marine life have often taken me onto – and into – the water around our coasts. I quickly came to realise what the sea is capable of and how quickly conditions can change. To know that there are these skilful, courageous volunteers ready to launch to your rescue at a moment's notice is incredibly reassuring and humbling when you're afloat or diving.

But there's another reason why I admire the RNLI's lifesavers. I love the fact they are prepared to preserve the lives of animals as well as human beings. That principle has always been important to me, ever since I was a child. We lived in a smallholding, surrounded by animals that my parents had rescued. Their approach to conservation – that all life is precious – shaped my values and my career.

As you'll discover in these pages, the RNLI's crews and life-guards have gone to the aid of all sorts of wild animals over the years, from seabirds and deer to a humpback whale. There's a fascinating range of stories waiting for you, and if you love animals I know you'll really enjoy reading this book. It's also wonderful to know that it will help to raise the funds that equip and train the lifesavers, ready for the next rescue.

INTRODUCTION

by Mark Dowie, Chief Executive of the RNLI

To save every one' – this is our vision at the RNLI. When our volunteer crews and lifeguards head to a lifeboat station or a beach patrol, they are driven to rescue *every* person at risk from drowning – not just *some* of them. These remarkable women and men keep people safe across the UK and Ireland, whether the call for help comes from inland waterways, beaches or the open sea. In fact, RNLI crews and lifeguards have saved more than 142,500 human lives since the charity was founded in 1824 – from swimmers and surfers to sailors and fishing crews.

Occasionally, our lifesavers are called to rescue animals. They respond for two reasons: one, because they are decent folk who feel compelled to save pets, livestock and wildlife as well as their fellow humans. But there's a humanitarian reason too. If a pet owner, farmer or concerned passer-by knows that a creature is in difficulty, there's a chance that they will enter the water to attempt a rescue themselves. As a dog owner, I can identify with anyone who would instinctively head into the water to rescue their cherished pet – my own dog Toby was fortunately rescued by the RNLI a few years ago. But these animal rescues can – and have – led to tragedy. As such, many of the rescues you'll read about in this book have indirectly saved human lives.

Whatever the rescue and whoever needs our help, the RNLI will respond, provided our lifesavers have the kit, training and support to keep them ready. That is impossible without the income that ensures our charity remains afloat. Thank you for buying this book and supporting the RNLI. It makes you a lifesaver too.

THE MOST POPULAR DOG IN CROMER

*As told by Jacqui Palmer,
RNLI Henry Blogg Museum,
Cromer*

In the late 1920s and 30s the small coastal town of Cromer was something of a magnet for British holidaymakers. Its beachfront was a picture-postcard scene come to life, with waves breaking gently on the golden sand, children in tin boats excitedly netting shrimps in the shallows and men relaxing in striped deckchairs as the smell of fresh Cromer crab wafted on the breeze.

This idyllic scene, set against the backdrop of grand Edwardian seafront hotels, would play out daily under the watchful eye of the Cromer lifeboat crew. Despite its undeniable beauty, the coastline at Cromer was renowned for its darker side. Its unpredictable and powerful tides, winds, currents and rock-hard sandbanks had claimed thousands of lives over the years.

For this reason, the town's lifeboat crew were respected and celebrated, and when their vessel, the *H. F. Bailey*, was on display, it was an attraction in itself. Locals and tourists alike would stroll along to marvel at her.

As they did so, more often than not, the boat would be flanked by a man in a flat cap with a large shaggy grey dog sat contentedly at his side.

The man's name was Henry Blogg and he was coxswain at RNLI Cromer. Henry had joined the crew at the age of 18 in 1894 and 15 years later won the vote to become coxswain, but the sea had been in his blood long before then. At 11 he had left school to work on his family's crab boat. When he wasn't out at sea, he could be found on the beach, hiring out bathing dresses and towels for a penny a piece.

Henry was a modest and private man, but if you were lucky he would sign a postcard or share a story. He certainly had a few to tell – none quite so enduring as a shout received in October 1932, where he first met his canine companion.

On Friday, 14 October the coastguard had sent word that a vessel had run aground on Haisborough Sands, and Cromer lifeboat had launched at 9.30am. Coxswain Henry had set a course for Mid Haisborough Buoy, and arrived alongside the stranded vessel – the SS *Monte Nevoso* of Genoa – at around noon.

On boarding the Italian steamer, which was carrying 33 crew, Henry conferred with the ship's captain, Angelino Solvatore.

'We've been aground since 4am,' the captain explained. 'We're going to try to refloat the vessel.'

The weather was calm and clear, and the chance of the boat becoming a wreck seemed remote, so as the tugboat *Noordzee* prepared to tow the *Monte Nevoso*, Henry and the Cromer

RNLI crew stood by, alongside five other tugs, ready to provide assistance. But as the hours passed and the vessel remained stuck, the moderate winds began to pick up.

By 5am on Saturday a gale-force wind from the north-west brought a heavy sea. The weather turned rapidly. Two of the tugs broke their tow and another was forced to cut its ropes. Just over 24 hours after running aground, the captain of the *Monte Nevoso* sent out a message.

Ship in danger.

Two hours later, after the Cromer lifeboat had been forced to weigh anchor three times and move into deeper water, another message was received.

Ship leaking. Two anchors out. Cromer motor lifeboat alongside. Probably abandon ship.

With all the tugs cast off, Henry and his crew swung into action, weighing anchor once again and veering alongside the vessel. One by one, crew members leapt from the *Monte Nevoso* to the lifeboat as it rose on the waves. In a heart-stopping moment, one misjudged the distance and plunged between the stranded vessel and the *H. F. Bailey*, but was swiftly hauled out of the water by the RNLI crew before he came to any harm.

One hour later, with 29 of the boat's crew and one from the *Noordzee* safely on board, Henry urged the remaining men – the captain, chief mate, chief engineer and wireless operator – to abandon ship as well. But they refused.

Reluctantly Henry left, but only to get the rescued men to safety.

After 30 hours at sea – ten of which had been spent in pounding seas and appalling conditions – Henry and his men landed the 29 crew members safely on shore at Gorleston. As they picked up some dry clothes and refuelled, Gorleston lifeboat's honorary secretary approached the coxswain.

'Would you like us to relieve you and your crew of the second trip?' he asked.

'No, thanks. Our job is only half finished, and we'll finish it,' Henry replied.

Back at Haisborough Sands, tugs were still standing by, waiting to resume towing as soon as the weather improved. The gale had subsided and the captain entertained fresh hope that the *Monte Nevoso* might be saved, but Henry was still concerned for the crew's safety.

'Please, captain, leave the ship,' he said. 'You can do no good by remaining on board.'

To Henry's astonishment, the captain once again refused.

'My radio is all right. If I need assistance I will send for you,' he said.

Henry reluctantly accepted the captain's decision and returned to Gorleston, staying the night at the Mariner's Refuge just half a minute's walk from the boathouse, in case the *Monte Nevoso* should send out an SOS.

The call never came, so at 5am on the Sunday morning, Henry and his crew headed back out to the vessel, flanked by two tugs.

The scene that greeted them was as bad as any he could have imagined. The vessel had broken its back and its funnel was below the waves. The four remaining crew were gone, but there was a glimmer of hope.

The steamer's motor boat was nowhere to be seen.

Henry weighed up the scene.

Perhaps they left of their own accord, he thought.

It was likely, but Henry wasn't one to do a job by halves, so the crew boarded the ship to carry out one final sweep. As they searched, they heard a whimpering noise coming from one of the cabins. It didn't sound like someone shouting for help or someone crying. It didn't even sound like a person. It sounded like …

'It's a dog!' one of the crew said gently, so as not to startle it.

Sure enough, there were a few passengers on the boat that had not previously been accounted for: several songbirds in cages, and not one but two dogs – a small black Terrier and a much larger, grey dog that the crew believed to be a St Bernard at the time. Guessing that they had been taken on the voyage as company and companionship for the men on the *Monte Nevoso*, the Cromer crew decided to rescue the animals.

They quickly removed the caged birds to the lifeboat and then sought to convince the two dogs to make the jump from the *Monte Nevoso*. The smaller of the two would not leave the boat and eventually scurried away into the wreck, but with a little encouragement the big grey dog leapt over and was brought back to Cromer Lifeboat Station.

On returning to the station, Henry learned that the captain and his remaining crew had abandoned ship at around 9 o'clock on the Saturday night, as the vessel split into three pieces and began to rapidly break up. Using flares to attract attention after the motorboat's petrol supply ran out, the four men had been rescued by a nearby trawler called *Gleam*. They had made the heartbreaking decision to leave the animals behind as they didn't think they would be allowed to land the foreign animals without formal quarantine arrangements in place.

The *Monte Nevoso* was never recovered, but the epic 70 nautical miles and 52-hour operation made local and national headlines, owing to the safe return of its 33 crew – and the news of a rescued dog.

It was reported that the rescued birds had been distributed among local people. But as astonishing photographs of 29 rescued crew members standing together in Yarmouth circulated, there was still one question on many lips.

Where was the dog?

That question was soon answered. The Cromer lifeboat crew had handed him over to the police for quarantine when they landed on shore. Henry was praised for his faultless seamanship, courage and endurance, but it was six months later when further news of the dog emerged. He was released from quarantine and as a mark of thanks, the vessel's captain gifted Henry the dog, which contrary to initial thoughts was later believed to be a Tyrolean Mountain Dog.

Henry – who had never owned a dog before – immediately renamed him.

Monte.

The *Monte Nevoso* rescue earned Henry a Silver Medal for Gallantry from the RNLI and a Canine Defence League medal for saving Monte. But perhaps the greatest gift was

Monte's companionship. Following the rescue, the pair were inseparable and could often be found sitting beside a beach hut or walking along the shore together. Countless photos capture the two together, often with Henry's wife Annie.

Monte quickly became the most popular dog in Cromer.

When people saw Monte heading towards the sea, barking and tugging at his lead, they would smile and suggest that maybe he wanted to get out to sea again, but it was clear where he was happiest. By his master's side.

From the moment Monte had leapt from that wrecked ship onto the lifeboat, he'd been Henry's dog. No one knew how old Monte was, but it was clear he was in his later years. Docile and calm, despite his great size, he learned to offer a paw and 'shake hands' with female admirers and excited children when he was out with Henry on their daily walks. A true gentleman, like his owner. He was also perfectly happy to sit at his master's feet while he engaged in long conversations with people around town.

When the pair weren't out walking together, in the summer months Monte would sit on the promenade watching Henry, Annie and their daughter Queenie looking after the bathing huts and chairs on the beach, while he was petted by many who passed by him. Henry's illustrious career on the lifeboats and the fairy-tale ending for Monte gave them both a certain celebrity status, in Cromer and beyond. When the next lifeboat day rolled around, Henry and Monte were given pride of place in the middle of the lifeboat as it was pulled through the streets of the town.

Poking his head above the shoulders of Cromer's lifeboat crew, contentedly accepting their scratches and tickles, Monte played up for the cameras. Local children pressed up to the side of the boat, arms outstretched and eager to pet the famous pup.

Everybody wanted to play with Monte.

And he was happy enough to oblige. After what must have been a terrifying ordeal for Monte on board the *Monte Nevoso*, his life in Cromer was comfortable, pampered and safe – save for one near-miss on the lifeboat slipway in July 1933.

Henry had taken Monte to the station, as he was going to join the crew on the *H. F. Bailey* as it was taken down to Rowhedge in Essex for an overhaul. Monte was to stay on shore, as usual. But as Henry boarded and the lifeboat was about to be launched, Monte wandered onto the slipway. Apparently undecided about whether or not to follow Henry onto the lifeboat, the dog had put itself in the path of the very vessel that he was rescued to. But at the last moment, as the boat was about to be released, an eagle-eyed onlooker spotted the unfolding incident and called Monte to safety.

Like so many special companionships, though, Henry and Monte's was significant but short-lived. In June 1934, two years after Henry rescued him from the *Monte Nevoso*, Monte passed away. Henry and Annie had taken him out for an afternoon walk just before Henry went out to sea. When he returned, he learned the devastating news that Monte was gone.

The next day the sad story made the local newspapers and the whole town mourned the loss of 'Cromer's most petted resident'. But none more than Henry. He was a man of few words who shunned the limelight, despite his great achievements, so it was Annie who spoke publicly of Monte's passing.

'His death was unexpected, and it has upset my husband,' she told local reporters. 'We had grown so fond of Monte. He was one of the family and practically my husband's best friend. We shall never have another dog. Not one could take Monte's place.'

Henry remained as Cromer coxswain for the rest of his career, serving an incredible 53 years and being the most decorated lifeboat crew member in the RNLI's history by the time he retired, aged 71.

He never did get another dog.

Seven years later, he joined his old friend Monte. Although both are gone, the tale of their friendship and how they came into one another's lives endures today, as do many, many myths.

Some say that Henry would take Monte out on shouts, but we know that he was far too professional and focused on the job of saving lives at sea for that to have ever happened, so Monte stayed safely on shore for the rest of his days. Others believe that after his death, Monte was preserved by a taxidermist, and when the RNLI Henry Blogg Museum opened many years later, some thought – and still do – that it was the real Monte on display. This, of course, is not the case. It's a mannequin dog made to look just like him (although sometimes we do tell people that our 'Henry' mannequin is stuffed too, just for a giggle).

When we have groups of children in, we get them to re-enact the *Monte Nevoso* rescue, passing a toy lifeboat around the room to symbolise the long journey and trying to pull one of our volunteers off the floor, just like the tugboats tried to pull the boat free. Then, at the end, a toy version of Monte the Dog is 'rescued' from a box. There's always the most enormous cheer when he's released and everyone gets a cuddle!

Just as Monte was a gift to Henry, he's a gift to the RNLI as well. He helps us to teach young visitors about the work our crews have done and continue to do. He allows us to teach them about bravery, about staying safe at sea and knowing that there are always people there who are willing to answer a call for help: incredible RNLI volunteers just like Henry Blogg – and his dog Monte, of course!

2

USUALLY
FRIENDLY

*Clare Cocks, Terry Jeacock and Vince
Jones, Moelfre, February 2017*

It was early evening on a calm Saturday in February and my daughter Beatrice, my partner Terry and I were out enjoying a lovely walk in the Anglesey countryside. Life had been quite stressful for us as a family. Terry had been in a serious road traffic accident in 2012, which had taken its toll on his mental and physical health. His recovery had been slow and we all needed a break from the hustle and bustle of daily life. An overnight trip to a beautiful cottage in the middle of nowhere had seemed just the ticket.

So far, it was doing the trick. We'd brought our two dogs Flossy and Chester (a Bichon Frise-Shih Tzu and a Bichon Frise-Pug mix) with us as well. As we walked along the clifftop path, they were pulling on their leads and inquisitively sniffing everything they found. Our pets were as much a part of the family as any of us and the break just wouldn't be complete without them. If we'd had room for our three cats – Oscar, Daisy and Lily – they would have been there too, but they were at home, being looked after by my mum, Judith.

We'd been out for a while and were heading back towards the cottage to have dinner. As we walked inland and away from the cliff edges, we took the dogs off their leads so they could stretch their legs. They bounded off excitedly, chasing one another and exploring their new surroundings. With our phones locked away in the cottage, we were completely disconnected from all of our daily stresses and strains.

It felt wonderful.

We took in the views and the country air as the dogs played happily together in front of us. Then, all of a sudden Flossy darted in the opposite direction, with Chester in hot pursuit. I couldn't tell if something had caught her attention or she was just having a mad moment, but as we looked behind us we saw the pair bounce over a raised grass mound and then disappear. Immediately, we called them back.

'Chester! Flossy!' I shouted.

Chester bounded back first and we waited for Flossy to follow. The two of them were inseparable, so when one appeared the other was never far behind. But more than a few seconds passed and Flossy still hadn't emerged from behind the grassy mound.

'Flossy!' I called again.

'She's probably found something interesting to sniff and investigate,' Terry said as he put Chester back on his lead. 'Flossy! Come here, girl!' he called.

Still nothing.

I frowned. It wasn't like her to ignore us when we called. She was completely bonkers and full of energy, but she was obedient too.

'Something's wrong,' I said to Terry.

'Let's go and take a look,' he replied.

'You stay back,' I said to Beatrice. I didn't want her too near the cliff edges. 'We'll go and see what she's up to.'

Terry and I made our way to the mound and peered over. As we did, we both gasped. A cove was cut into the cliff, bringing the edge far closer than it looked from a distance. Panic rose immediately in my chest.

'Flossy has gone down the cliff!' I shouted to Terry.

'Let's just have a look,' he said. 'Beatrice, will you hold Chester?'

As he passed the lead to her he sounded calm, but I could tell he was just as worried as I was.

Where else could she have gone?

While we could see the cliff edge, we couldn't see over it. I couldn't hear Flossy barking or whimpering either. My stomach lurched. I didn't want to look over because I was terrified about what I might see.

Flossy injured. Or worse …

But I had to know. I inched forward carefully, stomach churning. In my head all I could think was, 'Please let her be OK,' but I knew there was a big drop and there were rocks at the base of the cliffs. I wasn't holding out much hope. As I looked over the edge, my heart raced as I took in the height of the cliff. I steeled myself and began scanning below, searching for any sign. Then I saw her.

'There she is!' I shouted to Terry.

She was at the bottom of a sheer drop, stuck on a ledge at the very base of the cove. She didn't *look* injured, but how could I tell from so far away? And even if she wasn't, what would happen if she tried to scramble up herself and fell again, this time into the sea?

She might get swept away.

'I'll go down,' Terry said immediately.

'But there's no way down,' I said.

'There must be,' he replied.

Lying flat on his stomach, he inched further towards the edge, trying to see if there was any way at all to get down. Just the sight of him so close to the edge made me feel sick.

'Be careful,' I gasped.

'Why didn't one of us bring a phone?' he cursed.

'I know, I know,' I said. 'But there's no way down, Terry. It's too dangerous.'

He carried on frantically searching for a safe route. But there was none. I shook my head.

'What's happening?' Beatrice shouted, her voice shaking.

'Flossy's fallen but she's going to be fine,' I said, fighting to reassure myself as much as her and Terry. 'But we're going to need to get some help.'

Suddenly, I remembered passing a cottage on our way out. It was the only house we'd seen on our walk. The people who lived there would be local and might know a way to get down there, or at the very least I could use their phone.

'I'll run back to that house and see if they can help,' I said.

Then I looked directly at Terry.

'Don't try to go down and get her. I'll get help,' I said. 'You stay here with Beatrice.'

With Terry's health the way it was, I knew that it would be quicker and safer if I went, and as much as Terry adored Flossy, I knew there was no way he'd leave Beatrice in the middle of nowhere on her own, especially not with night falling.

'OK,' he said.

After making sure the three of them were safely back from the cliff edge, I started running, the blood pounding in my ears, keeping rhythm with my feet on the ground. I ran and ran until the house came into sight.

I sprinted up the path, then knocked urgently on the door, chest rising and falling rapidly with the exertion. A man opened the door and looked at me, surprised.

'I'm sorry, I wonder if you can help,' I said. 'Our dog has fallen from the cliff and is stuck on a ledge and we don't have our phones with us.'

It struck me as soon as the words tumbled out of my mouth. Phone or no phone, who was I even meant to call for help?

'Do you know if there's a safe way down to the bottom of the cliff?' I asked. 'We're not from round here and we don't know the area.'

'You can only reach it by boat, I'm afraid,' he said.

'Oh,' I said, stomach sinking.

'You should call 999,' he said. 'Ask for the coastguard.'

The thought hadn't even crossed my mind.

'Thank you,' I said. 'Where should I say we are?'

Using his local knowledge, the man gave me a detailed description of where Flossy was.

'Thank you,' I said.

Our cottage was a few hundred metres away from the house, so I turned on my heels and started jogging towards it to go and get my phone, even before the man had time to offer me his. Despite my panic, I was conscious that I was a complete stranger knocking on his door at nightfall and I didn't want to trouble him, not after he'd been so helpful.

Minutes later, I burst through the cottage door, grabbed my phone and dialled 999 immediately.

'Which service do you require?' the operator asked.

'Coastguard, please,' I said.

When they answered, I explained what had happened and exactly where we were, but in the back of my mind I couldn't help wondering whether they'd really come out for a stuck dog.

'Is there a risk that anyone might try to retrieve the dog themselves?' the coastguard asked.

'My partner is looking to see if there's a safe route down,' I said. 'I don't know if you help animals, but I don't know who else to ask. I'm just worried we will never get her back.'

'Please don't worry, we'll send a crew now,' he said. 'Just make sure everyone stays back from the cliffs and wait for us to get there.'

'Thank you,' I said, before hanging up. A few minutes later, the coastguard team pulled up outside the cottage.

'We will follow you to the location,' one of them said.

I dived into my car and led them to where I'd left Terry and Beatrice. When I arrived I jumped out and ran up to them.

'The coastguard is right behind me,' I explained.

The blue lights quickly appeared and the crew came running towards us. They had equipment that would help them descend the cliffs and they started looking for a way down, but it quickly became clear that it was too dangerous even for them to attempt. My heart sank again as a member of the coastguard team explained that the only way to get Flossy would be from the water.

'Don't worry,' he said. 'We've alerted the RNLI and they're sending a small lifeboat out.'

'The RNLI?' I said, surprised. 'They do that?'

'It's safer than any of us trying,' he said.

I understood completely, but I was still terrified. It felt like an eternity had passed and now there was hardly any daylight left. Even worse, it was getting colder and wetter. Poor Flossy was stuck down there all alone, possibly injured, and soon it would be pitch black. As we waited, one of the crew gave Beatrice their walkie-talkie.

'You'll be able to hear the lifeboat crew talking to us on that,' he said.

We strained our ears to listen for any news. As we waited, I knew we were all thinking about Flossy and what she meant to us. She was such a gentle soul, loved sleeping during the day and getting belly rubs from anyone who would give them. If you dared stop before she wanted you to, she'd playfully wave her front paws until you relented and started again.

No one could resist that move.

Chester would be bereft without his best friend, and what would life be like for us without her mad half-hours, her rolling in fox poo on long walks and her snaffling 'human food' – especially cheese – at any given opportunity? My heart wrenched in my chest.

'She has to be OK,' I pleaded silently to myself. 'She has to be.'

Standing in the pitch dark, our wait was agonising and felt like it would never end. Until all of a sudden, just over the cliff edge, we saw a light.

'It's the lifeboat's searchlight,' Terry said. 'They're here.'

I was in the kitchen at home getting tea ready for the family when my pager sprang to life.

Beep Beep. Beep Beep.

As always, its shrill, repetitive tone set me on alert immediately. I quickly wiped my hands on the nearest tea towel and grabbed the pager to read the message.

Launch ILB.

RNLI Moelfre on the island of Anglesey, where I worked as a full-time mechanic, covered a busy and varied coastline. We had both an all-weather boat and an inshore lifeboat (ILB), and we looked after the area from Puffin Island to the east of the station, all the way round the coast to Cemaes Bay. There were sandy beaches, steep cliffs, shingle beaches, marinas and ports, and the coastline was used for work and leisure in equal measure.

As a result we were called to all kinds of shouts. During my 19 years as full-time mechanic and 21 years as crew, I'd seen broken-down ships and injured seamen on board commercial vessels, helped beached porpoises, attended dinghy and jet ski rescues, and rescued dog-walkers unexpectedly cut off from land with their pets. The tidal surges, deep waters, short, choppy seas and jagged rocks could easily catch anyone out, even with years of knowledge and experience.

As I rushed to grab my car keys and headed for the front door, I spotted our eight-year-old Jack Russell, Tiz, dart across the hall and bolt up the stairs. A few years earlier, when I'd had a big old Land Rover, she would have been at the door waiting. I'd let her hop in with me and she'd sit minding the car while I went out, waiting excitedly for me to return. But my new car had a little less space for her and she was getting older now too.

But when the pager went, she still understood what was happening.

Knowing there would be a mad chaotic rush to get out the door, she'd move out of the way so she wouldn't get under my feet. She was a good girl like that. Our two cats, Tink and Tigs, probably lounging in the big dog bed in front of the fire that the three of them shared, were pretty well rehearsed too.

As I jumped into the car and started the engine, my mind turned to the job at hand. It was a dark February evening, so it wasn't likely to be a leisure-related shout, although at this time of year there wasn't much fishing going on either. More often than not, when we received a request to launch in winter it was something serious.

Better get there fast.

A couple of minutes later I was in the station and kitting up. We had a visiting coxswain at the time and he was huddled together with some of the local crew, deep in discussion. I didn't know what it was, but something about the mood in the boathouse made me realise that this wasn't going to be an ordinary shout.

What an earth could it be?

I joined the rest of the crew to be briefed on the information the coxswain had received from the coastguard. It emerged that a three-year-old female had fallen from the steep cliffs at Porth Wen about eight miles along the coast.

A three-year-old female Bichon Frise.

It wasn't a life-or-death kind of shout at that moment, but the fact that our casualty was a dog didn't lessen our pace. We knew that if someone was really determined, there would be little to stop them from making an attempt to rescue their pet,

23

and then the situation could change in a heartbeat. It certainly wasn't going to be an easy job either. Port Wen was a disused brickworks at the foot of a sheer 40-metre drop.

The coastguard rescue teams from Cemaes and Holyhead were already on the scene, but it was too risky for even the local cliffs team to try and get down to retrieve the dog. Getting to her by water was really the safest option.

It was nevertheless still a treacherous stretch of water and our approach required some real thought before we left. Putting our £2.7 million all-weather lifeboat out on the job wasn't practical or wise. But our inshore lifeboat *Enfys* was ideal for navigating the rocky outcrops and shallow waters near the beach where the pup was stuck.

'How are we going to capture the dog?' one of the crew asked.

It was a good question. We didn't have any specific animal cages or pet slings at the station, but we certainly didn't want a scared and unwieldy dog inside the boat with the crew.

'How big is the dog?' someone asked.

'Only small, apparently,' the coxswain replied.

'What about one of our drysuit bags?' I said. It was the perfect solution. They had a nice big opening at the top that we could coax the animal into, there was space for it to move its legs around and we could secure it in there as well.

'Let's do that,' the coxswain said.

I was asked to helm, and our trainee helm, Michael Hughes-Roberts, and another young crew member, Robert Jeffrey, were picked as well. I knew it was going to be a challenging shout, not just on account of the unusual casualty, but because it was a tricky area to navigate the ILB around safely.

With the coastguard teams on the scene to prevent any potentially risky moves by the dog's owners, we decided it would be a good opportunity for our trainee helm, Michael, to lead on. It was cold and dark but the weather was fine, and he would be able to take charge of the boat preparation and navigation, with me overseeing.

We had time to take a breath, but the adrenaline was still the same because people, animals and the sea have one thing in common.

They are all unpredictable.

Everything could change in a moment, so we were never exactly sure what would meet us at the scene.

Was the animal injured and agitated?

Would the weather turn?

Would the owners panic and risk themselves to save their pet?

'Let's do a quick briefing before we go,' I said as we headed to the lifeboat.

Once on board, we went through our plan to get into the gully where the dog was stuck and decided how we would retrieve her when we got there. Like me, Michael had dogs too, so I knew his experience with animals would help when we found the pup. As we launched down the slip and powered out to sea, we received further information from the coastguard on the animal's location.

'I can confirm it's on the eastern side of Porth Wen Bay. The dog is supposed to be very friendly. Over,' the coastguard said.

'What is it called?' I asked.

'Lassie.'

'Lassie?' I said, frowning.

Our stuck pup was named after the hero dog that was always on the scene to help someone in trouble?

Surely not.

I picked up the radio.

'Just to confirm, it's called Lassie?' I asked.

'Flossy. Flossy,' came the reply.

'Ah, it's Flossy,' I said to the crew.

'Flossy, usually friendly. Over,' the coastguard said again.

Well, it was good to know the dog was usually amenable. But we couldn't be too complacent. I was usually friendly, but I'm not sure how I'd be if I'd just fallen 40 metres over a cliff.

Twenty minutes later, we were approaching the east side of Porth Wen. We'd lost a lot of light and had to slow down to navigate through the big outcrops of rock and reefs in the bay. Once again, I started considering all the variables.

Where was the dog now?

Where were the owners?

What condition was the dog in?

Using the light from the boat and our head torches, I guided Michael in towards the beach.

'Come in to port, mate, yeah?' I said.

'Yeah,' he replied, completely focused on the task at hand.

'Engine off,' I said, as we reached a couple of metres from the shore.

'Engine off,' Michael replied.

It was time to go ashore and see what we were dealing with. I went ahead to assess the situation. Standing in the shadow of the cliff, it hit home just how far she'd fallen. The owners must have been horrified. No doubt they were in a right state now, waiting for news. I knew exactly how I'd feel if it were Tiz.

I'd be beside myself.

I turned back to the boat.

'You all right if I go up there, Mike?' I asked, ensuring he was comfortable keeping the boat in position.

'Yeah, all right,' he said.

I grabbed the drysuit bag, pulled on my gloves and waded the last couple of metres to the beach. It was pitch black, so I called back to Rob.

'Can you follow me with the searchlight?'

'Yeah,' he shouted, jumping from the boat and illuminating the path ahead of us.

It was rocky and pools of water lapped around our feet, making it slippery underfoot. I looked on the ground for the dog first and listened for something barking or whimpering, but I knew any noise might be drowned out by the sound of the waves crashing against the rocks.

'Look, up the cliff,' Michael said through the radio.

I started scanning up from the beach and along the craggy cliff side.

Then I saw her.

A few metres ahead of us, up a natural embankment, was a little white dog wearing its lead harness and collar, sitting on a ledge jutting out from the cliff about 10 or 15 feet up from the beach.

'I can see her!' I shouted.

She looked bedraggled and scared, and she was very, very quiet.

My heart sank a little. That wasn't a great sign.

Maybe she was injured.

Robert adjusted the beam of the searchlight to illuminate the dog and I started calling out to her, as gently as I could.

'Hello, dog,' I said. 'Hello, doggy, there we are!'

It was a little bit like talking to a child. I just wanted to keep her calm. In the beam of our searchlight – and now also illuminated by a spotlight provided by the coastguard from above – I could see she was shaking. She raised her head suspiciously and I immediately recalled all the training I'd received about approaching a scared dog.

Don't put an open hand out to it.

Don't look at it directly.

Turn your back to it.

You see, I knew I was there to help, but she didn't.

The dog didn't know me and I didn't know her, so we were going to have to take this easy. After about five minutes of inching forwards, I knew I was well in her line of vision.

What was she seeing?

A big alien-type creature hulking towards her in a yellow suit, red lifejacket and helmet. No wonder her eyes were as wide as saucers. The poor thing must have been petrified.

'Hey, hey, hey,' I soothed as I inched closer.

For the life of me, I couldn't remember her name.

Was it Fluffy?

Hearing the low rumble of a growl that was building up inside her, I thought better than to call her the wrong name.

Better stick to 'dog' for now ...

'Hello, dog. Hello, dog,' I repeated in my lowest, gentlest tone.

I didn't have a fear of dogs, I respected them and knew they responded to tones of voice. I needed her to know I was here to help. But she wasn't convinced. As I neared her, she raised her little head and let out a high-pitched howl, then she started to bark.

Bark bark. Grrrrrr. Bark bark. Grrrrrr.

As she yapped and growled, she started to move around on the grassy ledge she'd found herself stuck on. It was good to see that she seemed relatively uninjured, but this presented another challenge.

She was going to be harder to get down.

'OK, visors down,' I said to Rob.

The last thing we wanted was an angry little Bichon Frise lunging towards us as we scrambled up the rocks to reach the ledge. It was a case of visors down, get the bag ready and be prepared for anything.

Once I was on a steady footing, I took the bag and opened it.

'There we are,' I said gently, as I moved forward with it.

But as soon as I did ...

Grrrrrrrrr. Yap yap.

She snapped angrily towards my hand and I pulled it swiftly away. It was as if she knew my game.

'There, there,' I tried again.

'Usually friendly'? I thought. *Yeah right!*

Then again, after a fall like that I don't think anyone or anything would act like they normally would. I tried to move

29

in again. She had nowhere to run and all I had to do was get her in the bag.

Easier said than done!

'Shhhh, shhhh,' I soothed, offering her the back of my gloved hand so she could have a little sniff, hopefully convincing her that we were friendly humans. She calmed down a little, but as soon as we moved closer her mood changed again.

As we started trying to coax her towards us – and the bag – she burst into a cacophony of barks, yaps and growls, snapping wherever my hands went. She wasn't having any of it.

That's when I knew.

There was no way we'd be able to convince her to come to us. She wasn't going to come nicely. She was telling me who was boss.

And it wasn't me.

I stopped, looked at her and shook my head.

I wasn't going to hang around a cliff being told what to do by a Bichon Frise!

There was only one thing for it.

I knew from owning a dog how to grab one safely, so I just had to wait for my moment. I let her bark and yap for a minute, and just stood by. Then the second she looked away I took my chance. Moving swiftly like a ninja, I grabbed her by her scruff, and lifted her up off the rock and above the bag.

She was not *amused.*

Writhing and kicking her back legs in anger and nipping at me, she barked and wriggled, desperately trying to evade the opening of the bag. I tussled with her, and eventually managed to get her back legs and torso in. But her front paws were still fighting. Eyes wider than they'd been since we arrived, she let out something between a hiss and a growl. It was clear she was terrified. Popping her head in and zipping the thing up would have been the most practical option, but the pup had already had one heck of a day. I didn't want her scrabbling around in the darkness with no idea where she was going, so I decided to leave her head sticking out.

That way it would be a bit less distressing.

With a little more wrestling left and right, I managed to get her front paws in the bag and quickly swooped in to secure the zip snugly around her head.

She was in!

'OK, I've got the dog!' I shouted.

Carefully scrambling down the cliff, we made our way back to the boat. As we navigated back through the rocks, the dog's head poking out of the bag and growling away, Robert spoke.

'Just watch that she doesn't make a run for it,' he said.

'She's quite comfy in here, I think,' I said, looking down.

But for how long?

It took us two minutes to get to the boat. The dog seemed to have calmed down, but as I lifted the bag on board and climbed in myself, I wanted to be sure.

I didn't want any of my crew injured by her.

Or her running off into the sea.

'I'm going to have to try and secure the bag a bit better, guys,' I said, sitting down.

As Michael started taking us back to the station, I turned my attention to the petrified pooch, who was now on my lap in the bag.

'Hello, Floppy …' I said.

Then I paused. Was that right?

'… or whatever you're called.'

I was just glad to have her safely on board.

I radioed the station and the coastguard immediately.

'Just to confirm, we've got the dog in the bag here. All safe and well.'

While we'd been rescuing the dog, the coastguard had been with her owners at the clifftop and I knew that this simple message would be a huge relief.

Then I picked the radio up again.

'Quite the opposite of friendly,' I chuckled. 'But that was probably to do with the faces of the two we sent ashore. We'll meet you in Bull Bay.'

It was much closer than the lifeboat station and the coast-guard would be able to get the owners down there easily to be reunited with the dog, rather than extending their worry. As we set off, I put the bag on the seat next to me and looked down. The dog was no longer struggling and was staring up at me.

'Those eyes look like you want to eat me,' I laughed.

During the five-minute journey, I kept popping my head down and talking to her, making sure she was OK. I think she knew that she was safe, but low growls made it clear she still wasn't very happy.

You're not my mate yet, mister.

I couldn't blame her really.

Before long, Bull Bay was in sight. We stopped the boat at the shoreline, climbed out and, with the much calmer dog now fully zipped up in the bag for extra security, made our way towards the rescue crews standing together at the shoreline.

Among them I could just about make out three members of the public: a man in a dark jacket, a woman in a white padded coat and a young girl, all looking anxiously at me – and the bag.

Her owners.

As we reached the pavement where they were waiting, I grinned at them.

'How are we doing?' I asked.

'We're fine, how are you?' the man in the dark jacket replied. I raised an eyebrow.

'Friendly, my –' I said, cutting the sentence short as we all burst into laughter.

'She was supposed to be friendly?' asked Robert.

The man was called Terry and he introduced himself, his partner Clare and her daughter Beatrice.

'Was she a handful?' he asked, pointing to the bag. 'We heard some barking over the radio.'

'She was fine,' I said, waving my hand away with a smile, before placing the now-wiggling bag gently on the ground. I didn't want them to worry. The poor creature had been so terrified, I wasn't surprised she'd lashed out a bit.

'Just be careful when we open it as she might be a bit scared and disorientated,' I said.

As I held the bag towards them, Terry started speaking gently to the dog.

'It's me,' he said. 'I'm here, it's all OK now.'

33

I opened the bag slowly – a pile of soggy white fur was just visible through the opening. Terry leaned over, her little head popped up and she started excitedly licking his face, tail wagging inside the bag.

'Here, Flossy,' said Terry, picking her up and wrapping his arms around her.

That was it! Not Fluffy or Floppy. Flossy!

'There you go, Flossy!' one of the rescue team said. I swallowed a little lump in my throat. It was hard not to feel emotional as Clare and her daughter, Beatrice, stepped forward and drew Terry and Flossy into a tearful group hug.

It was a lovely moment to witness.

You could almost see all the terrible things that had gone through their minds just floating away. Flossy was a completely different dog to the one we'd met on the cliff ledge too.

Now she was calm and in her owner's arms, I offered the back of my hand to Flossy.

'Hello, dog,' I said. This time she nuzzled into me. 'There we are,' I said as she allowed me to give her a little scratch around the chin.

'Thank you so much,' they said, over and over.

You could feel the sense of relief they were experiencing and I completely understood it. As we chatted, it emerged that Terry had started looking for ways to climb down to find her, but Clare had discouraged him.

His reaction wasn't unusual. Although it would have been the worst possible decision, I completely understood how his love for his pet made him consider descending the cliff himself. I know many others that would have done the same. But I was glad Clare had convinced him otherwise.

Watching them being reunited, you could see that the dog was a part of the family. The emotion was overwhelming to witness, almost exactly the same as reuniting a family with a lost child.

With Flossy safe on dry land, we said our goodbyes and took the boat back to the station to prepare her for her next service. As we were pulled up the slipway, I radioed the coast-guard: 'That's us back on slip and closing down.'

Once all the usual checks and maintenance were done, I put the drybag-suit-cum-dog-carrier in storage, jumped into the car and headed home.

Job done.

Sitting on the sofa, I reflected on the day. There was no doubt it was incredible that Flossy had survived such an enormous fall and escaped completely unhurt. Although it was just another rescue to us, it was much more than that in so many ways. It was another life saved and a family reunited.

I felt a huge sense of pride. It was always nice to do good.

Not long after I returned home, Tiz wandered into the room.

'Hello, Tiz,' I said.

Instinctively, she jumped onto the sofa beside me, to welcome me home.

My wife looked over. Tiz wasn't allowed on the furniture so she'd usually be chased off the sofa. But tonight I wrinkled my nose and shook my head.

'Come here, girl,' I said, scratching behind her ears as she made herself comfy.

Just for tonight, we'd let her off.

Although it was all a bit of a blur, I don't think any of us will ever forget the moment that we were reunited with Flossy. We'd heard snippets of the rescue over the radio and knew they were bringing her back in, but until we actually saw her it was hard to feel relief. As soon as she was out of that bag, though, it was such an incredible atmosphere. Relief and happiness all around. The crew asked if they could take a few photos of Flossy, and I just remember us all thanking them over and over again for their efforts.

Once we got Flossy back to the cottage, Terry gave her a bath and checked her over for any injuries that might need attention from a vet, but she was completely unscathed and, apart from being a bit tired, she was acting perfectly normally.

It was like nothing at all had happened.

I think the whole ordeal affected us more than her and Chester. The next day we were on the beach and she was desperate to run around, but we weren't quite ready to let her off the lead again. The experience has made us think more about our surroundings with the dogs, because with hindsight we know that it could have been avoided. One thing that particularly stuck in Terry's mind was something one of the crew said when they brought Flossy back to shore.

'It's nice to have one of these with a happy ending.'

We know just how lucky we were that the RNLI were there and able to come to help Flossy. We had been naïve letting the dogs loose in an area we didn't know, and our story could have had a very, very different outcome. It really brought home how important it is to be very careful when exercising dogs in unfamiliar areas – and to keep your phone on you! We just hope our experience will prevent others from making similar mistakes. We really cannot overstate just how much it meant to us that the RNLI went out and saved Flossy, and how grateful we are for their brilliant work. Because of them, our family is still complete and Flossy is back to her old tricks, snaffling our cheese and begging for belly rubs.

③

A 'MIRACLE' AT PORT TALBOT

Ashley Jones, Port Talbot,
November 2017

It was a grey Sunday afternoon when the call came in from the coastguard – Sunday, 5 November, to be precise, with the smell of fireworks from the Bonfire Night festivities the night before still clinging to the breeze. After more than 20 years as a volunteer at RNLI Port Talbot, it would be safe to say that the crew and I had seen it all.

While some stations along the coast tended to deal mainly with commercial rescues or holidaymakers in trouble with local tides, our patch meant we never really knew what kind of assistance might be needed. The station looked after an area that contained three rivers, a beach popular with locals and tourists, an inland freshwater dock, the Port Talbot depot that served the local steelworks, and a whole host of marinas. Our bread-and-butter shouts tended to be missing children, fishermen who found themselves in difficulty and a fair few animal rescues. It wasn't unusual for marine wildlife to find itself stuck or for dog-walkers to need our help to retrieve pets that had got stuck in precarious positions.

In many ways, the day started just like any other.

'There's an incident down at the west end of the prom,' the coastguard said. 'Some sort of animal trapped. The RSPCA is already there.'

'We'll get down there now,' I said.

'It looks like a tricky one,' he added. 'You might be in for a long haul.'

The call hadn't come as a surprise. Port Talbot is a close-knit community so we'd already had word from members of the public, such as the dog-walker who thought he'd heard a dog barking in the same area. Information had been filtering through on social media and through local news reports too.

I heard what sounded like a baby crying down there.

It's an animal stuck on the beach.

Looks like it was scared into hiding by the fireworks.

I heard something yapping away, the poor thing. Is anyone going to help it?

As word spread, a crowd had started to gather. While it was heartening that the local community was showing such concern, when an animal was trapped we knew there was always a risk that well-intentioned members of the public would try to help and find themselves in trouble as well.

We put the call out to the rest of the crew and within minutes the station was full. The coastguard was already out there with the RSPCA, but we had our Land Rover and other kit that might be useful in helping get the poor stuck creature back to safety, not to mention crew to manage the incident from a sea-safety perspective.

A few minutes after the call, we were on our way.

When we arrived at the scene we found RSPCA and wildlife rescue crews huddled around a pile of boulders about 200 metres from the sea. I walked over and one of the RSPCA team spotted us.

As they made their way towards us to update us on what they knew, I heard a faint, pitiful yapping noise emerging from a gap among the rocks. I frowned. It didn't sound like a dog, not even a small one. It was more guttural; in fact, it sounded like a …

'It's a seal,' the RSPCA officer said. 'We have a seal pup stuck under a boulder.'

'How did it get down there?' I asked.

'We don't know,' he said. 'But it's really jammed in there.'

'Let's have a look,' I said, as we reached the boulders.

The group stood back, and I squatted down and looked into the gap. Peering back up at me, about four foot down, were two big, sad black eyes.

'Oh dear,' I said.

It really was stuck. It looked to me like it had fallen in and found itself pinned in place by one of the rocks. Whatever had happened, it hadn't got in there intentionally, that was for sure.

'You're in quite the situation there,' I said.

It was away from the sea, hungry, distressed and dehydrating rapidly. There was only so much help we could give it while it was stuck. There was the issue of the tide too. If it came in, we'd have no access at all and although the seal was stuck above the tide line, if there was a big groundswell, the water could rise above the tide line and drown the poor thing.

We were situated in Bristol Channel, which has the second-highest tidal range in the world, and a spring tide was

43

on the way. These came in much further than neap tides, so that risk of the water rising was even higher than usual.

As it was, there was no way it could wiggle to free itself, and the tiny gap meant there was little chance a human would be able to squeeze in and get it out. Even if they could, the boulders easily weighed a couple of tonnes each, so we'd need to get kit in there as well, to help lever them off the pup.

I stood up, took a step back and scratched my head.

What are we going to do here?

Our crew had rescued many an injured or stranded seal in their time, usually after a storm had washed them up on shore, but I'd never seen one in a position that was quite as tricky as this.

'We're going to have to lift the boulder off it,' I said.

Quite how, I wasn't sure.

'Maybe we could use a crane?' someone suggested.

'There's no way to get one down here with the incoming tide,' I said.

There was a small car park nearby that might have acted as a base to work from, but it was too far from the incident site to be feasible. What we needed was something that would allow us to lift the boulder up, a structure of some kind that would sit over the incident area and allow us to strap up the boulder and lift it clear, so the RSPCA could get in and whip the animal out.

'Are there any other options?' I asked.

'Well, if we can't get it out before the tide comes in and the water starts to rise, there's only one,' an RSPCA volunteer said. 'To make sure it doesn't suffer.'

Putting it down.

44

A knot tightened in my stomach at the thought. I didn't want that to be the conclusion we came to. Looking at the faces around me, no one else did either.

That had to be a last resort.

There was no quick solution to the situation and whatever we decided needed careful and effective planning. The coast-guard had been right.

We were in for a long haul.

I turned to one of the RSPCA officers.

'If your team leads on the animal welfare, we'll lead on the extraction,' I said. 'But we're going to need some extra help.'

After fully assessing the site and checking the tides, we made a decision. With the tide still out, the poor pup wasn't in immediate danger. But the operation that was needed to get it out would take time to set up. Once it was prepared, we knew we'd probably only have one chance to get the seal free.

We contacted engineers from Associated British Ports and Sea Lift Diving, local contractors who had the kit and expertise to help us move the boulder. They met us on the beach and we thrashed out the logistics. The bare bones of the plan were to bring the lifting kit to the site, set it up and hoist the boulder away.

But before that, we had another challenge to navigate. News of the stuck animal had spread far and wide – Franco's, the local fish and chip shop, was even sending fish down to the RSPCA officers so they could feed them to the seal pup.

When we left the scene to prepare for the next day, from the outside it looked as if we were abandoning the pup. Social media and the town's streets were awash with comments.

Why are they just leaving it there?

The poor thing can't just be left to die, surely?

Someone has to do something!

It couldn't be further from the truth, but we were unable to share full details of our rescue plan as we were still working them out. We closed off the beach from the prom area, about 150 metres from the seal, and the RNLI communications teams pushed out messages to reassure people that we were still working hard to help her. The local RSPCA even put out a press statement.

> Access to the seal is exceptionally difficult. We are
> awaiting the opinion of specialists to see what
> engineering options may exist to help the seal. We would
> urge anyone in the local area to remain at a safe distance
> and not seek to access the seal at this time.

But the worry that stark warnings might not be enough was never far from our minds. In a way, that was what spurred us on even more. Planning ran through the night with the RSPCA, contractors, engineers and the divers from Marine Life Rescue. I don't think anyone grabbed more than a wink of sleep, but by the following morning we were ready to try to free our little friend.

We cleared the area ready for the arrival of the gear and the RSPCA did further health checks on the pup, to make sure it was wise to progress. One tide had been and gone, and the water hadn't risen too high, but there was a bigger tide on the way, so time was of the essence. The seal was still distressed and dehydrated, crying out every now and then, but at least now it had a full belly thanks to the feast provided by the local chip shop!

At midday on the Monday, more than 24 hours after the seal was found, the lifting gear arrived.

Now all we had to do was set it up and get the little pup out, right?

If only it were that simple. With around 30 contractors and volunteers from the various rescue agencies, we had the inshore lifeboat and full crew on the water in case anyone got into difficulties. There was lots of heavy equipment being lugged about and generators dotted around too, so we needed crew to keep curious and concerned public away from the scene, not to mention to support the work of our press officer, Mel Cooper, and keep the media updated on progress.

My main job was to coordinate everything and keep *everyone* safe.

Including the seal pup.

The size and shape of the equipment meant it couldn't be brought down ready to use but had to be assembled piece by piece over where the seal pup was stuck. The gantry pieces were driven in a wagon as far onto the beach as they could safely reach, then we carried the two legs and crane arm over to a concrete pad that was surrounded by the large boulders where the pup was trapped. It had previously been used as a helicopter landing pad and was about as close as we could get the kit set up.

Once we'd shifted the lot over, the engineers got to work constructing the frame into a sturdy arch, with a block and tackle usually used for lifting heavy construction materials and boat engines.

Stage one, complete.

But we still had a way to go.

The beach was full of jagged sea-defence boulders. It wasn't a case of just rolling the gantry into position, as there was no clear route through. We all swung into action again, laying boards across the boulders, so the gantry could be moved over the gaps between them. When it was all together, the thing was as heavy as the boulder that we needed to move, so if it slipped and got jammed, we'd need another one to lift it out.

If that happened, we'd run out of time to help the seal.

We had to be slow and precise.

Once we got the gantry over one boarded section, we took the boards left behind and lay them in front, inching slowly forward until eventually it was positioned right over where the pup was.

We huddled together with the engineers for an update, ahead of moving on to the next stage of the plan – securing the lifting eyelets into the boulder.

'How are we doing this?' I asked.

'We'll need to drill into the boulder and secure the eyelets with cement,' he said.

'OK then, let's do it,' I said.

As the engineers prepared their industrial drills, I liaised with the other agencies, making sure that everyone understood what was happening next, checking everyone was fed and watered, that the shifts were relieved so crew could get some rest and checking with the RSPCA about the implications of using drills near the animal.

'It's going to get a little noisy,' I advised.

'We'll keep an eye on the seal and let you know if we need to stop,' the RSPCA officer said. We both knew there was really no other way, but if we could reduce the pup's distress in any way, we'd do everything we could.

Just before the engineers got to work, I popped my head over the gap.

The poor thing was still sitting there, in exactly the same position, its big, scared eyes staring up, snout and flippers obscured by the boulders above. It must have wondered what the heck was going on.

I wonder if it knows we're here to help, I thought.

'We're working on getting you out, you silly thing,' I said gently.

Although it had cried a lot at the start, it must have exhausted itself. It barely moved, save for its chest rising and falling rapidly as it panted away.

As the hours passed, we began to lose light and we knew the tide would soon be coming back in. Understanding that the job was going to be a long one, I'd liaised with teams to ensure we had lighting, so we could keep working into the evening and night if we needed to.

By the time the lifting eyelets were in place and the hoist chains from the gantry had been wrapped around the boulder and hooked on securely, more than five hours had passed. We were all exhausted, but determined too.

All that was left to do was lift the boulder.

We needed to act slowly and precisely again. If we moved too fast and the boulder slipped and fell down onto the pup …

I shook my head.

We'd got this far. That didn't bear thinking about.

As the lift started, the chains extended and the air vibrated with the sound of metal against rock. I held my breath.

Was this contraption really going to work?

Slowly – ever so slowly – a gap started to appear. My heart was racing, but it seemed to be holding. Every minute that passed, the gap became a few millimetres bigger and the tension in me eased by a similar-sized fraction. There was still no room for error, but it felt like we were getting somewhere.

Then, about halfway through the lifting process, the hoist began to sway. I watched in horror as the boulder started to give, the top half splitting away from the rest of it, possibly weakened by the drilling.

No, no … I thought, heart sinking into my stomach.

As the sound of crashing rock echoed around the beach, I clenched my teeth together and looked away. When I looked back, the boulder had dropped some way. Suddenly someone shouted.

'Everybody stop! Everybody be quiet!'

For a moment, it was as if we were all frozen, listening for any sounds from the exhausted pup.

I wasn't hopeful.

That's it, I thought. *Game over. The seal is squished.*

An engineer ran over and peered down the hole and I steeled myself for the worst. But when the engineer turned round he was smiling.

'It's all right!' he shouted.

An audible sigh of relief rippled across the beach as the engineer turned his attention to the now precariously positioned rock. Boosted by the good news, I made my way over to the team for another update, as the seal's fate hung – quite literally – in the balance.

It was a far from ideal situation.

The boulder's position had moved during the lift, so if we put it back down and started again, there was every chance it would crush the seal. If we carried on lifting as it was, the bit of the boulder that had broken away would fall onto it.

'We'll fit some strops around it to secure it,' one engineer said.

'And carry on from there?' I asked.

'Yes,' he nodded.

'Right then,' I said.

In for a penny, in for a pound.

New strops in place, and with engineers positioned nearby with crowbars to help ease the boulder through tighter spots, the lifting started again. The wait was agonising, but millimetre by millimetre we moved closer to the end goal. After hours and hours of slow and steady work, we knew that once the boulder was shifted we'd have to move quickly.

After such a long ordeal, we couldn't just put the seal back out to sea, so we had a travel box at the ready to put it in and the RNLI Land Rover on standby, so we could take it straight

51

to be checked over by the RSPCA vet, before deciding what to do next.

We were all poised and ready to go.

After an hour of slow and painstaking lifting, the boulder was high enough to be shifted to one side. Once it was safely moved away and the OK was given by the engineers, it was all systems go. An RSPCA member pulled on his protective gloves and helmet, took an extending noose and climbed into the hole as we stood by with the travel box open. I didn't envy them one bit. As cute as baby seals are, they could be nasty and have a vicious bite.

Right now, speed was of the essence.

Dipping the noose down, he expertly secured it around the pup and started pulling it up, but it didn't come easily. After hours of exhausted silence, it was now barking and crying, and you could hear it thrashing around aggressively.

Who could blame it?

Being dragged out of the darkness onto a floodlit beach surrounded by dozens of people must have been terrifying. Rescuing people, you could always talk to them and calm them down, but the poor pup didn't have a clue what was happening.

As the RSPCA member got it to the opening, he grabbed it by its scruff and passed it up towards the cage.

After a final wiggle and thrash of its tail, we had it.

'It's out!' someone announced, and the cage door was fixed behind it.

After more than seven hours of incredible teamwork, the seal was free.

There might have been a collective cheer, but I don't remember, because we were already on our way over to the

Land Rover with the travel case and our unwilling passenger in tow.

'Let's get you checked out,' I said, over the racket.

Despite the two-day ordeal, the seal pup was unharmed and even earned itself a nickname – Miracle. Throughout the operation we'd called it a few choice names, especially when the tiredness had kicked in, but given the happy ending, Miracle certainly suited it.

Once the seal had been given the once-over, it was taken to a specialist facility, the RSPCA's West Hatch Wildlife Centre in Taunton, Somerset, to recuperate fully before being released back into the wild. But our job wasn't quite over.

At 8pm, the Port Talbot lifeboat was launched once again to Aberavon Beach.

The structure we'd erected needed to be dismantled and moved, and the boulder needed to be shifted back into a safe position, so the engineers and contractors were still hard at work on top of the boulders. At the same time, the tide was coming in and strong winds were churning up a rough sea.

Our job wasn't over until *everyone* was safe and the area was clear.

We provided cover for just shy of an hour before returning to the station to wash down the boat and prepare it for its next service, then it was home to bed.

Over the next couple of days we received updates from the sanctuary about how Miracle was doing. Turns out the seal was rather unfazed by the whole thing. It was rehydrated and had started to put weight back on too – something I think the local fish and chip shop may have contributed heavily to! It was lovely to hear after everyone's efforts. The good news was all over the press too, keeping Mel particularly busy.

Once all the fuss had died down, despite the fact that the rescue was one of the most challenging and technically complex we'd been involved in, it was back to business as usual for us. Every now and then we'd see bits and bobs in the press saying that Miracle was still in the sanctuary and doing well, but we really didn't expect to find out much more.

Then, one day, one of the crew spotted a news story online.

'Look who it is,' they said.

I scanned the article.

A female seal trapped by boulders has returned to the wild.

After six months of being cared for at the sanctuary, where the staff had renamed her 'Marina', she had been deemed a healthy enough weight to go back into the wild. She had been released at Combe Martin in north Devon, with seven other rehabilitated seals for company.

Glancing at the accompanying photo – a seal's head poking just above the waterline, big black eyes fixed on the camera – I smiled.

I recognised that little face.

She might have had a new name, but she was still definitely our Miracle.

4

A BLACK CAT'S LUCK

Mark Pusey, Chiswick,
June 2020

Volunteering at one of the two busiest lifeboat stations in the country, it wasn't unusual to find yourself out on a shout almost as soon as you came on shift. Like RNLI Tower a few miles further down the River Thames, Chiswick is crewed 24 hours a day, 7 days a week, 365 days a year, so we are always able to launch to an emergency within seconds.

I first got involved with the RNLI as a child when my family moved to Exmouth in south Devon for a few years. We lived a few minutes from the lifeboat station and we'd go down to the seafront as a family to watch the boats launch. We helped with fundraising, went to open days, and I even had a photo of myself at six years old, all kitted up in a safety helmet, old lifejacket and RNLI wellies.

As a born-and-bred Londoner, technical diver and freelance session musician, I found being a member of the RNLI crew on the river a bit of a dream, and it fitted in well around my work – or the lack of it after COVID-19 hit in 2020. Like plenty of people, I hadn't even realised there were lifeboat stations on the river until by chance I saw an article online, but once I knew, I was set on joining, even if there was a waiting list. I finally joined the Chiswick crew in 2018.

The variety of the work was astonishing. The Thames is always busy, with all kinds of vessels travelling along it, and people and pets on its bridges, footpaths and foreshores. We'd regularly be called out to towing jobs and medical evacuations – fires on houseboats, people in mental health crises, and those ending up injured or ill in places that were difficult to get an ambulance to – as well as individuals and vessels that had been caught by the tidal flow of the river and found themselves in trouble.

But it wasn't always people we had to go out to. We saw our fair share of animals in distress too.

I'd only just stepped onto the pontoon on Sunday, 7 June 2020. I was in my drysuit and on my way to do our usual boat checks with fellow crew member Steve Law when I noticed about 20 or 30 people looking down from the barriers onto the foreshore. We were a few months into the pandemic, so seeing lots of people out taking their daily exercise wasn't unusual, but seeing them gathered in a crowd – albeit socially distanced – was.

'What's going on there?' I said to Steve.

Steve squinted ahead, shielding his eyes from the sun.

'Seems like they're looking down at something on the fore-shore,' he said.

The tide was coming in, so even from a distance I could see that the piece of land that usually ran along from Chiswick Gate was rapidly disappearing. I ran down to the boat and grabbed the binoculars to get a better look.

58

As the scene came into focus, I could see people pointing down towards a family of ducks at the water's edge, circling something just a few feet away from them. Then I spotted it: a small black creature huddled nervously against the river wall.

Hang on, was that a …?

'Steve, it looks like a cat,' I said, passing him the binoculars so I could get a second opinion. As he lifted them to his face, the small figure moved.

'Yeah, that's a cat all right,' he said

'Cats aren't swimmers, are they?'

Steve shook his head.

Growing up, we'd always had pets. My parents had a cat called Jess when I was a baby, so I couldn't say I'd been a cat owner, but I knew enough to know they weren't fans of the water, not to mention how much affection people had for them.

We'd seen it countless times. Dogs and cats weren't just any old animal to people. They were a beloved pet to a child, a companion to a grandparent, an irreplaceable part of a family. When a household pet was in trouble, more often than not someone would go in to save it. Owner, bystander – it didn't matter; the drive was the same. But usually the animal would self-recover, and it would be the person that ended up in serious trouble.

That was the last thing we wanted to happen.

I did a quick calculation in my head. Right now the cat still had a patch of dry land. But the tide was coming in and would be rising at a rate of about two centimetres a minute. In five minutes it would have risen by about ten centimetres.

About the height of a cat.

If we didn't get there quick, the poor animal would be toast. Suddenly I was on high alert. I was an animal lover and had no desire to watch the poor thing drown. I also knew it was only a matter of time before someone decided to go down onto the foreshore and try to save the thing themselves.

I picked up the radio and called the boathouse. Our commander, James Anthony, was on duty.

'James, we have a cat stuck on the foreshore and a big crowd watching it,' I said. 'The tide's coming in. Shall we go and get it?'

'I'll call the coastguard,' he said.

Within moments we had the coastguard's go-ahead. Like us, James knew that what was unfolding could become a much bigger emergency if we didn't act immediately.

The lifeboat station was easily visible to the crowd, so as we dashed up the pontoon to grab the rest of our kit people started waving and pointing, as if to say, 'Hey, where are you going?'

But we were back in seconds, joined by James and Tony Coe. Usually when we launched, we didn't know what was awaiting us at the scene. We'd have basic details from the coast-guard and would be planning for all eventualities. But on this occasion, as we climbed into our E-class lifeboat we could see exactly what was happening and we knew it was salvageable, so the mood on the boat was relaxed and everyone was in good humour. No one joins the RNLI to sit around in the boathouse, so it felt good to be going out on something a little bit different.

We arrived on the scene in about 90 seconds. As we pulled up alongside the foreshore the ducks scattered in a flurry. A knowing nod from James told me that I'd been volunteered to get out and grab the cat.

It made sense. I was in the drysuit after all, and although I wasn't *new* crew, I *was* the *newest* member. I wouldn't say I'd drawn the short straw, but as I stood up, I realised I had absolutely no clue how to handle a cat.

I turned around to the guys.

'Does anyone know anything about cats?'

Three heads shook in unison. There wasn't a cat owner among us. Although we had RNLI protocols and processes for animal rescues, every species was different. I'd had dogs growing up and was the proud owner of a double-maned lionhead rabbit called Mufasa. At least I had some frame of reference there, but a cat?

Not much at all.

I turned round, climbed off the lifeboat, took a few steps onto the foreshore and then stopped to look closely at the ball of fur jammed into a corner of the river wall. Its big, scared green eyes stared right back at me. Although I couldn't see a collar, it was clearly a well-fed and well-looked-after cat. A family pet, not a stray.

Meow, it whimpered.

It was terrified. Of course it was.

A massive red boat had just sped up to it and I'd jumped off. In my yellow RNLI kit, red lifejacket and white helmet I must have looked like a big space monster bearing down on it.

And I was supposed to calm it down?

I was going to have to try. I pulled my visor down and took another step forward.

'Hiya, little one,' I said gently, giving a little whistle. 'It's OK.'

The cat remained flat, head to the ground but still eyeing me suspiciously.

Hisssssssssssssss.

I tried to make myself smaller, crouching to the ground to be nearer its level. The cat raised its head and looked around, but I could tell it wasn't welcoming my presence. It was clearly nervous, on edge.

I looked around too. We were about 500 metres from Chiswick Gate, where the foreshore was accessible at low tide, and there was another entrance point about 300 metres away. It had probably wandered down for a nice little stroll or to chase the ducks and had been having a perfectly lovely time until it tried to turn and go home, only to find it had been cut off by the tide. It wasn't going to just bound over to me and leap into my arms, so I had to think.

How was I going to get it on the boat?

Ideally, I'd do it without the poor thing ending up in the water or scaring it too much.

'Have you got a blanket?' I called back to the crew.

Steve was already there, holding out the famous navy-blue RNLI blanket.

'Do you want to wrap it up?' Steve said.

'Yeah, just so I don't get scratched to hell.' I was wearing gloves and protective gear, but that didn't stop me from worrying. I could tell that whatever approach I tried, the cat wasn't going to come easy. It was going to fight me and might just catch me with its claws.

I unfolded the blanket as I walked back towards the cat.

'All right, little one,' I said as I opened up the blanket. 'It's OK.'

I received an angry 'meow' in response and I saw its fur stand on end. I was trying to soothe it, but standing over it, arms outstretched and holding a massive piece of material, I wasn't fooling anyone.

I think it knew exactly what was coming.

As I crouched down, instinctively I whistled again. It jumped to attention, reared up against the wall and sort of yapped at me. It was a sound I'd never heard a cat make before. Its two front paws were poised, ready to dart away.

'It's OK,' I said, pulling back slightly.

But now it was in a standing position and on high alert, wondering what this big human was up to. I turned back to the rest of the crew.

'It might just have to be a throw and grab –' I shouted, before I was interrupted.

Meowwwww, the cat cried.

It was almost as if it had understood me.

'You're going to have to get the blanket on it,' James called back.

I took a deep breath and gently dropped the blanket over the cat, but its head immediately popped out from under it, standing paws up against the river wall and giving me an accusatory stare.

What are you trying to do to me?

I paused for a second to let it settle. I knew what I had to do. I had to get the blanket over it, pounce, wrap it up and get it in the boat.

You can do this, I told myself.

This time I had to be faster.

'Do it now!' someone shouted.

Taking another deep breath, I threw the blanket over it again, this time crouching straight down to grab it, but the cat still had other ideas. Wriggling free of my hands, as if propelled by a surge of adrenaline, it started scratching frantically up the side of the river wall.

It was like trying to grab hold of a bar of soap.

Quickly collecting myself, I grabbed its back legs and pulled it back to the ground before throwing the blanket over it again, this time grabbing it around its middle.

Got you!

I turned on my heels and started heading towards the life-boat, my arms outstretched, offering the cat to the waiting crew. Steve was preparing a second blanket to grab it, but James wasn't quite so keen.

'Don't give it to me!' he said, eyeing the razor-sharp claws that were peeping out of the blanket in his direction. The cat was hissing and squirming, but I had it in my grip.

Or so I thought.

Suddenly, somehow, it managed to wiggle its front legs completely free and was frantically clawing at the air, twisting left and right trying to pull away from me and back towards the river wall.

'Woah!' I said.

Before I knew what was happening, it had wriggled around onto its back, facing me – claws out – with its paws in a boxer's pose. The expression on its face said it all.

What are you playing at, mate?

It wasn't going down without a fight. As I struggled to keep hold of its lithe body, I'd never been so glad to have my visor down. It was terrified, writhing and scratching at me, its teeth bared and hissing angrily.

Then all of a sudden my hands were empty.

What the …?

Before I had a chance to wonder where it had gone, I felt claws hooked onto the shoulder of my drysuit. The cat was on my back! As I was about to reach up to it, I felt paws down my other arm and then … nothing.

'Where is it?' I shouted, dizzy from the flurry of activity.

'It's back on the ground!' someone shouted.

I spun around, and sure enough, the little rascal had wriggled free, run around me and was now back on the rapidly disappearing foreshore. Laughter rippled from the crowd above – and from the lifeboat.

It was like something out of a Tom and Jerry *cartoon.*

Only this time the cat was outwitting me!

Was it time for a new strategy? The throw-and-grab method clearly wasn't working and the cat was onto me now, in any case. This time, instead of settling back down into its sheltered position against the wall, it started stalking away towards the direction of the lifeboat station and the end of the remaining bit of foreshore.

I watched and frowned. There were only two or three metres of dry land left now, so maybe I still had a chance to grab it. I followed slowly behind, blanket outstretched, ready to pounce again. After all, cats hated water.

Surely it wouldn't willingly enter the river …?

Every few seconds it looked over its shoulder at me, meowing, as if to say, 'Leave me alone!' but sure enough, as it reached the edge of the water, it stopped and retreated back against the wall.

I moved fast, dropping the blanket over it and grabbing it from behind.

'Wrap it securely, mate!' I heard someone shout from the lifeboat.

For a moment, I had it.

The cat looked at the river ahead, and then looked back at me. In that moment I knew exactly what it was thinking.

I'm going to have to swim for this.

It pulled away, legs squirming from my grip and kicking the blanket off, before darting straight into the river with a splash. Bounding once, then twice, paws creating ripples around itself, it probably felt quite smug, but on its third bounce the water suddenly became deeper.

With the ground out of its little paws' reach, its entire body was immersed within seconds, four legs paddling wildly and head straining to stay above the water. It was clear it was struggling, but panic had taken over. It just swam and swam, further and further out into the deeper tidal water.

Unlike with people in the water, there was nothing I could do to calm it down and explain how I could help. There was only one thing I could do now – wade in behind and wait until it was too tired to swim anymore.

I sloshed slowly in its wake, so as not to cause additional distress – or further annoyance. It was heartbreaking to see it desperately paddling to the river wall, hoping to find something to cling onto. But there was nothing.

Even going with the tide, the pace of its little legs started to slow. It was as if it suddenly realised there was no escape route in that direction, and about ten metres from the now-tiny patch of foreshore it turned around, only to find itself trying to swim against the tide. It was a challenge even strong human swimmers wouldn't dare take on. By the time I caught up with it I was hip-height in the water. Its little head went under once, then twice, then it looked up at me helplessly.

All its fight had drained away.

This time, as I dipped the blanket into the water and clasped my hands around its body and front legs, it didn't struggle. In fact, it tilted its head sideways towards me. Maybe this was its way of giving in.

OK, I actually need help now …

But still, I wasn't taking any chances. Before I turned back towards the lifeboat, I wrapped the blanket securely around that cat's soggy body, making sure its four legs were all contained, then closed the gap at the bottom by pulling the end up and tucking it in around its head.

It was a bit like swaddling a baby.

As I trudged back towards the lifeboat the animal hardly moved, just looked up at me every now and then. Checking up on me.

It was only when we approached the lifeboat again that it started to wriggle.

I looked at the cat and then at the lifeboat.

I needed to hop back on board, but that would mean having to use at least one of my hands to haul myself up. If I loosened my grip at all, or tried to pass the cat over to the crew, I knew it could slip away and the whole saga would start all over again.

'Is it easier for me to get on with it here?' I asked, gesturing to the swaddled feline. 'It's wriggling.'

'You should keep hold of it,' James said. 'We don't really want it getting loose on the boat.'

'OK,' I said.

'If you come here,' he said, patting the lifeboat, 'I'll hoik you in.'

'All right,' I replied.

I turned my back to the lifeboat and moved backwards until I was touching the side of the boat, with my arms down and clasping the cat tightly towards me. I felt James grab my life-jacket and hoist me up. As I did, I momentarily released my right hand and pushed up on the side, allowing me to quickly swing my legs back inside the boat.

One, two, grab the cat again, I thought.

Fortunately, it didn't try to make a dash for it this time.

'You just sit there with it,' James said.

I hadn't planned on doing anything else.

Safely on the boat, I looked down at the bedraggled mess that was now sitting in my lap, eyes wide, wrapped in a sodden RNLI blanket. The cat might have given me the run-around, but the poor thing was terrified. How could I be annoyed at it? I was just glad it was all right. Head poking out from the blanket, it looked around inquisitively but didn't try to run at all.

Maybe it knew it was safe now.

'There you go,' I said, gently tickling its head.

Suddenly, a ripple of applause snapped me out of the moment. It was the crowd of onlookers. I'd been so focused on grabbing the cat that I'd completely forgotten we had an audience. I looked over my shoulder. I couldn't tell if they were happy I'd finally got the cat, if the cheer was a little sarcastic or if they were just pleased I hadn't been killed by the angry little thing.

I'll take it anyway, I thought, smiling and giving them a thumbs-up.

Within a couple of minutes we were back at a nearby jetty. It was the quickest way to get the cat ashore. I was still clutching it tightly as we approached the gate at the top, when all of a sudden it started kicking inside the blanket.

Here we go again …

At least now we were well clear of the danger of the water.

It might have been that the cat recognised its surroundings, but it definitely didn't want to be held again.

'I think it might just go,' I said to Steve, as he held the gate open for me.

Before I knew what was happening, its front paws were out of the blanket and reaching towards the pavement as its back legs pushed my chest away. I leaned forward to put it down, but before I did, it leapt from my arms.

It was off!

For the fourth time that day, the cat had escaped my grip. But this time it was safely back on dry land and out of danger. I breathed a sigh of relief.

But it was short-lived.

No sooner had its paws hit the ground and sprinted off past a gated monument near the jetty than a brown dog nearby spotted it. I gasped as the dog gave chase.

'Oh no, the dog,' I said.

For a moment my heart was in my mouth.

Was the cat going to make it?

Fortunately, our feline friend, supercharged by adrenaline, was well ahead and easily outran the pup by a good 100 metres. Realising it was defeated, the dog tottered back to its owner.

Thank goodness!

I did wonder what must have been going through the poor cat's mind as it made its way back home.

I need a nap.

To be honest, after all its antics, I was just relieved that it was safely on its way back home to dry off and have a much-needed rest.

As well as crew, I was also a lifeboat press officer for Chiswick RNLI. I publicised rescues, water-safety messages and the work the organisation does by working with the regional, national and international press and doing media interviews, as well as sharing clips of our work on our social media pages.

This rescue had been so action-filled and unusual, it felt like a good one to share. People who had seen the cat in the water but might not have stayed to see us launch would know it was OK – and who didn't love an animal story with a happy ending? Even if it meant everyone seeing me struggling to deal with the slippery customer, it was a great way of showing the variety of our work.

I posted the video to Facebook and all of a sudden everything went nuts. The local newspaper wrote a story about it and before we knew it we had the *Daily Mail*, *Sky News*, Reuters and Associated Press on the phone. I spent the next three days doing interviews about the cat rescue. The headlines made the most of the bizarre situation.

Feline ungrateful! Stranded cat gives lifeboat crewman the runaround

Stranded cat does everything it can not to be rescued

Cat stranded on River Thames tries (and fails) to evade rescuers in London

There was something about the story that captured people's attention. Articles were appearing all over the UK press for days afterwards. Then I received a phone call from a university mate in Australia.

'I've just seen you on our news rescuing a cat,' he said.

'You're kidding!' I exclaimed.

The story had gone global.

Back in the boathouse, there was still plenty of talk about the rescue too. The ribbing I received could only be described in one way.

Relentless.

I didn't mind, though. Our little escapade, however comical and cartoonish, meant that no members of the public had ended up in the water trying to rescue the cat – and somewhere, somebody's pet came home safe and well, if a little shaken and soggy.

As the days passed, the station received piles of thank-you cards with cats on them from animal lovers around the world. Local cat owners stopped in with treats for us – and any future feline casualties.

'If you have any problems next time, just try offering them one of these,' one lady told me, holding out a bag of cat treats. 'They'll be right over to you.'

And something else happened. Donations to the RNLI came in thick and fast, to thank us for making the effort to go out for the cat. First it was hundreds, then thousands.

Then tens of thousands.

For an organisation that relies on public donations, it was an incredible boost and made the slight dint in my pride completely worth it.

We didn't really hear anything about the cat itself immediately after the rescue, but a few days later our shift was back in the boathouse when we saw a black cat strutting past the station. Suddenly it stopped.

'Hang on a minute,' I said. 'Isn't that …?'

Steve and a few of the other lads came to the window and the cat looked over, flashing a distinctive white patch on its chest.

'It certainly is!' I said, grinning.

The cat lifted its head towards the station slightly, perhaps in acknowledgement of our assistance a few days earlier. Then it turned away to carry on with its stroll. It was a great feeling. It looked much fluffier and had clearly had a nice long catnap.

'It must live locally then,' I said.

About a week after the rescue, we had that assumption confirmed. A family turned up at the lifeboat station with some tubs of cakes for the crew.

'We believe you might have rescued our cat,' the man said.

It turns out that the cat's owner, Nick Delmas, had seen the original rescue story in the local news a few days after it happened. When he'd seen the video, he thought the cat looked like their cat, Merlin.

Nick had been out on the Sunday that the rescue had taken place, but his son Etienne had been at home.

'Did Merlin come home wet on Sunday afternoon?' he'd asked.

'Yeah, he came back wet and I don't know why,' Etienne replied.

The feisty feline we'd rescued had indeed been Merlin.

As we chatted, the family explained how they lived a short distance from the station and had been long-time regular donors to the RNLI. Their generosity had played a part in saving their own pet and now, with Merlin's story going viral and generating donations, his rescue would enable us to help even more people – and pets – in the future.

It was a wonderful ending to a story that had really snowballed into far more than we'd ever expected and highlighted the importance of every single rescue – human or otherwise.

⑤

A GAME OF
PUFFIN AND
LIFEGUARD

Scott Brierley, Filey,
July 2018

I'd wanted to be a lifeguard ever since I'd been rescued by one at the age of 11, when I was swimming in the sea at North Bay in Scarborough. It was always a challenge to swim through the waves but I was a strong swimmer – I even competed – so I felt pretty confident out there.

I was happily swimming along when out of nowhere an RNLI lifeguard appeared beside me on a rescue board.

'Are you OK?' he asked.

Startled, I just nodded. Did it look like I was struggling?

'Let's help you back to shore,' he said.

Recognising my confusion, he explained that I was swimming along above a sandbank and was drifting out to sea on a rip current. I hadn't even realised. But apparently people often didn't.

That's what made the sandbanks and rips so dangerous.

'It's not a safe place to swim here,' he said. 'Even for strong swimmers.'

As he helped me back to shore, I realised the danger that I'd actually been in. It was a lesson that I never forgot. But what also struck me was how the lifeguard realised I was in trouble, even before I knew it myself. A few years later, when I saw a poster for a lifeguarding course up on a noticeboard in college, I signed up straight away.

I joined the RNLI lifeguards at Filey in 2016. It was quite a safe beach, because of its gradual slope and calm seas. Most of our work was delivering first aid on the beach and patrolling to keep an eye on people swimming in the sea, making sure that no one was going to get into difficulties. Like the lifeguard who spotted me, it was our job to spot potential issues *before* they developed into something serious.

Filey was also on a part of the North Yorkshire coast that was renowned for the animals that made their home there, such as seabirds, seals and porpoises. Quite often we had more wildlife problems than we did people problems. We'd be called out to injured seals and birds, both in the water and on land, and capture them so they didn't hurt themselves more. If they were out on the water it was important too, because if we didn't go, a member of the public would almost certainly take it upon themselves to attempt a rescue.

Once we'd rescued an animal we'd call the RSPCA or – in the case of any birds found – a local lady who ran a bird sanctuary nearby. They'd come along, pick them up, and if they weren't in too bad a way they'd nurse them back to health before releasing them back into the wild.

Although I had two dogs of my own that I loved, before I moved to the area I wasn't what you'd call a wildlife lover. Lifeguarding in Filey was a real eye-opener for me, and after three years of patrolling the shores I ended up liking wild animals almost as much as my own pets.

I was just as happy to go out and rescue an animal as I was a person, and I kept an eye out for both, especially if the seas were choppy. It was rare to see rough seas at Filey, but on Monday, 23 July 2018 we had about two to three feet of swell kicking about, so I was busy patrolling the beach, advising people not to go in the water. When I got back to our lifeguard station, Henry Baxter, our senior lifeguard, was staring at something ahead of him in the water.

'What's up?' I asked, following his eyeline to a patch of swell.

'I think a puffin's just landed in the sea,' he said, grabbing some binoculars.

'A puffin?' I repeated.

'I think so,' he said.

I knew there was a huge colony of puffins at Bempton Cliffs, about five miles down the coast, but they rarely ventured as far north as Filey. I don't think I'd seen one in my whole time working in the area.

'Is it struggling?' I asked, taking the binoculars.

'I'm not sure,' he said.

As I looked out to sea, I could see a distinctive, brightly coloured bill peeking out from a load of spray caused by the bird flapping its wings. It was definitely a puffin, but was it in trouble? It was hard to say.

Every so often it would bob underwater. Puffins were made for the sea. They could dive to great depths to catch fish to eat and were excellent swimmers. As the bird came up and started flapping again, I had a sudden thought.

I'd been an excellent swimmer, but I'd still got in trouble.

One thing I'd learned with animals was that if they got in the water they often self-recovered, especially when they'd evolved to live in or around the sea. If there was no risk of someone trying to be a hero, sometimes it was best to wait and see if they righted themselves without human interference.

But after about 20 minutes of monitoring the situation the puffin didn't seem to be doing any better. It kept going under more often and for longer periods. A crowd of people had started gathering against the beach's barriers too, watching and pointing in the bird's direction.

How long before someone tried to help it?

I couldn't leave it any longer.

'I'm going to go in and get it,' I said.

I had my personal wetsuit with me, which was a shorty and much quicker to get into, so I pulled it on and threw my yellow lifeguard T-shirt over the top.

I'll only be out a few minutes, I thought.

I mean, how hard could it be to scoop up a bird that was the length of a rugby ball and weighed just over a pound?

While I was preparing my rescue board, one of my supervisors came over from our support centre with a cage that the lady who took in the injured birds had left with us. Given the number of birds we picked up, it was always a useful thing to have lying around.

I jogged to the shoreline with my board and the cage. As the waves were rolling over my feet, I loosely tied the cage to the board so it would stay put but still be easy to manoeuvre to get the bird in.

Cage secured, I climbed onto the board and started paddling out towards our feathered casualty. It was only about 100 metres out, which was probably why it was in so much bother. Puffins usually dived for food way out to sea, not in the shallows. This one had clearly ventured too close to shore and was battling against the swell.

Momentarily, so was I.

As I paddled over a patch of swell, I felt the motion rock the board and the cage started to slip off. I quickly grabbed it with one hand and held on to it, using my other hand to pull myself towards the puffin.

A couple of minutes later I was there.

At the sight of me, the bird started flapping more, clearly scared of the large human in a bright yellow T-shirt looking over at him. I looked at the bird, then at the cage. Then I realised.

I'd come out without a proper plan.

I guess I'd expected to get out there, grab the bird, pop it in the cage and get back to shore. I thought that I might not even need to get in the water.

But the reality wasn't quite so straightforward. For one, the opening of the cage wasn't very big. I also had no way of letting the bird know I was there to help.

What was I going to do here?

Trying to grab such an agitated creature also put me at risk of getting pecked. It might only have been a tiny animal, but its big, bright beak looked like it could do some considerable damage.

I radioed back to Henry on shore and explained the state of the bird.

'Can you try scooping it up with the cage? Over,' he said.

'I'll have a go. Over,' I responded.

I climbed into the water and untied the cage from my board. I turned around and moved towards the bird, but as soon as I did it started snapping its beak and moving away from me. Then it disappeared underwater. I waited a moment, but it didn't resurface.

'Bird went under and it's not come back up. Over,' I said.

There was a pause, then the radio crackled to life again.

'It's resurfaced. In front of you, ten metres.'

I looked ahead and spotted it being churned around by the waves. I swam over and assumed a position to be ready to pounce with the cage. Then it disappeared again.

This time Henry was on it.

'Stand by. Over,' he said.

I waited for further instructions. From the beach and with the binoculars, they had a much better vantage point.

'To your right, five metres. Over,' Henry said.

I pulled myself around to the right and, sure enough, there it was again. But this time, before I had a chance to even move, a wave dragged him under. I scanned around, waiting for him to pop up again.

'In front of you, ten metres. Over,' Henry said.

It indeed was, but only for a fleeting moment. Then it bobbed underwater again.

Are you kidding me? I thought. Then Henry radioed again.

'It's behind you,' he began, then I heard him stifle a laugh.

I started to laugh myself as well. What was this, a pantomime?

It was starting to feel like one!

Henry coughed and composed himself.

'It's behind you, ten metres. Over,' he said, fighting to maintain an air of professionalism. To be honest, I don't know how he was managing it. I was in the thick of it and it was comedy chaos. I could only imagine what it looked like from the shore.

The game of puffin and lifeguard went on for about 15 minutes.

Then, at last, the bird started to slow down. As it did so, I saw more opportunities to catch it. I waited patiently until it was so out of puff that it didn't have the energy to fight, then I grabbed the cage, aligned the opening with the bird and scooped it up.

I lifted the cage out of the water.

It had worked!

It was in the cage, finally. I quickly shut the door in case it tried to dart out, and put it on my rescue board. The poor thing was waterlogged and absolutely exhausted, its chest rising and falling rapidly. But it was still clearly suspicious. It looked up at me and cocked its head as if to say, 'What are you doing with me?'

As if it hadn't spent the last 20 minutes making me chase it left, right and centre!

'Let's get you back to the beach,' I chuckled.

I secured the cage to the board again and radioed Henry.

'Coming back in. Over.'

I started swimming the board back to shore and the bird hardly moved an inch. Once the water was shallow enough to stand up in, I released the cage, picked it up and walked the rest of the way back in.

Henry had already called the lady from the bird sanctuary and she was on her way. She'd been as surprised as we were that we'd found a puffin in our area. We popped some fresh water in the cage and put it in the sun next to our lifeguard hut so the puffin could dry out a bit.

Despite having been fighting the swell for almost an hour, it seemed pretty content, so I started writing the incident report. It was more or less the same form as for people, but you just ticked 'wildlife rescue'. As I recorded the details, I started to laugh again. With the bird now safe and well, the hilarity of the rescue really started to tickle me. It was certainly a shout to remember.

Over the next few weeks, the lady from the sanctuary sent regular updates to the station about the bird. It was recovering well from its ordeal, and about a month later she sent a message to let us know that she'd released it back onto Bempton Cliffs.

Where it belonged.

I left the RNLI a few years ago when I moved areas. I'm a pool lifeguard now, so the chances of having to reuse my finely honed puffin-rescue skills are slim. The story still makes me laugh, but it's also a good reminder that if even the strongest swimmers and creatures that are adapted to the sea can find themselves in difficulty, anyone can.

STUCK IN THE MUD

Emily Jones with Ian Farrall,
Hoylake, April 2019

The lifeboat station at RNLI Hoylake was full when I arrived, a few minutes after our pagers had gone off. The coastguard had requested the launch of our hovercraft, the *H-005 Hurley Spirit*, as two horses and their riders were stuck in mud. Our coxswain, Andy Dodd, told us what he knew, looking directly at my crewmate Ian Farrall.

'You're hovercraft crew, Ian,' he said. 'And you too, Emily,' he added.

I knew exactly why Ian had been picked. He'd been with the RNLI at Hoylake for eight years, first as part of the tractor crew who helped launch the hovercraft and later as hovercraft crew. More than that, though, he knew an awful lot about horses.

As he tasked Matt Schank to be commander and Chris Green to be pilot – you 'flew' the hover rather than driving it – I looked at Ian and wondered if he was thinking the same as me.

Two horses? And two riders? And other people out there with them?

With that many potential casualties involved, there were so many scenarios that could be unfolding, including serious ones. To the world outside of RNLI crew, animal rescues often looked cute and even fun. This would be anything but.

He looked as concerned as me, but I was glad he was coming out. I had some experience working with large animals in my job as a firefighter, so I knew how anxious and temperamental they could be, but his specific expertise and understanding of horses would be vital for us on this shout. As we kitted up, we absorbed the information we'd received from the coastguard. The riders were young girls, accompanied by adults, who had got into difficulty on the coast near Leasowe in the Wirral. We knew the location well. It was a specific and extremely boggy stretch of mud that quite often caught people and their pets out, especially if they weren't familiar with the area.

Even if you were, it was a tricky place to navigate.

We served an area on a peninsula that exposed a huge expanse of mud when the tide was out. On top of that, we had a really fast tide. It went a long way out, which often gave people the impression that they were safe.

But it could be behind you in minutes.

It was so easy for people to find themselves standing on a sandbank thinking everything was fine, when the tide had actually come in and cut them off from land. It was one of the main reasons that our inshore boat was a hovercraft. We got it in 2016 and it was the perfect vessel for navigating the terrain we worked on, getting to casualties quickly without getting stuck ourselves.

I'd been RNLI volunteer crew since 2005. Growing up, I'd learned to sail in the Sea Cadets and by 16 I was crewing boats. That was when I had my first real interaction with the RNLI. I was a crew member on a boat that was being brought back from the south coast. Everything had started out fine, but as we were coming round the Bristol Channel the weather just blew up. We managed to get through the storm but the boat wasn't in a good way. Our engine failed and we'd taken on a lot of water.

Between bailing out and making very, very slow progress, we called the coastguard.

'We'll send the lifeboat out for you,' they said.

Although we were managing, it had been a frightening ordeal, so when the lifeboat came alongside us it was an incredible relief – just seeing the light, the lads looking over the rail and calling out to you.

Are you all right?

As soon as they were there, I was.

I knew I was in good hands and everything would be OK. The rescue made such a massive impression on my life. I never forgot the way I felt that second I saw the boat turn up.

It made me realise, I want to do that for other people.

So I did. The same drive paved the way for the career in the fire service that I chose too. About a year after joining the crew at Hoylake, I applied to be a firefighter. When I went to my interview, one question I was asked stuck in my mind.

'Why should we give you a job?' my interviewer asked.

'Well, I'm RNLI crew. I already work in quite a stressful environment, mainly male dominated, in the middle of the night, in difficult conditions. Why shouldn't you give me a job?' I replied.

They must have not come up with any reasons, because I got the job.

My volunteer role and day job overlapped quite a lot. We often worked with my colleagues from Merseyside Fire and Rescue Service, and today was no different. Along with the coastguard, they were already on the scene.

We climbed into the hovercraft and the shore crew pushed us out of the boat shed on the launch trailer. The hovercraft was launched in a different way to our big Shannon-class all-weather lifeboat, the *Edmund Hawthorn Micklewood*. Once we were out of the shed, our tractor driver took the trailer down the slipway onto the wet sands of the beach. With the trailer positioned head to wind – pointing the bow of the hovercraft into the wind – the straps were removed and the ramp and the back of the trailer were dropped. When everyone was clear, Chris turned the engines on and the fans kicked in, creating a cushion of air for the craft to sit on. Then we reversed onto the sand.

With a final push from the shore crew, we were off.

The location wasn't too far away. Flying across the sand and shallow water, engine throbbing like the sound of helicopter propellors, we looked around to see if we could spot anyone in the distance. Every second was spent watching and anticipating what might be waiting for us at the scene. We always went out with some information, but the situation almost inevitably changed. We had to be prepared for anything.

We launched at 10.26am. A few minutes later we spotted the blue lights of other emergency services, as well as two horses surrounded by people – some were rescuers, others the casualties that we'd been tasked to assist. As we approached, Ian pointed ahead.

'Look, one of the horses is walking to shore,' he said.

'Oh, that's great,' I said. 'At least one's out.'

A sense of quiet relief washed over all of us. Our job had just got 50 per cent easier. Obviously, getting a stuck horse out of the mud wasn't going to be a walk in the park. But it would still be far more manageable than getting *two* out. But that was really where the good news ended. As I scanned the scene, my eyes landed on the second horse.

Crikey! I thought.

The poor thing was stuck up to its armpits. Its legs weren't visible at all and the coastguard team were frantically using their gloved hands to dig around it.

'The poor thing's belly deep!' Ian gasped.

His reaction told me that this wasn't going to be a straight-forward job, based on the horse alone. And we still didn't know the situation with the human casualties.

'Looks like one rider is up,' Ian said. 'The other looks stuck.'

There were two girls, no older than 12, and two adults, presumably their parents or guardians. You could see one girl had been waist-deep at some point, from the muddy tidemarks on her trousers. The other appeared to be sitting on the mud, with a man digging around her leg. She didn't seem to be in any pain or distress, it just looked like the horse had gone down and her leg was stuck between the animal and the ground.

'She doesn't look injured,' I said. 'But let's get over there.'

Mindful of distressing the animal, Ian indicated to Chris to stop the craft a short distance from the scene of the incident. It was noisy and created a lot of draught, throwing a considerable amount of mud around, so we had to be careful about our positioning, not to mention our approach.

As we prepared to climb off the hover, I began to draw on my experience of other animal rescues. We'd had our fair share, usually dog-walkers cut off by the tide or with pups stuck on sandbanks that were unwilling to get in the water. As much as we loved animals, our main concern was to stop owners putting themselves at risk by trying to retrieve their pets.

Stuck horses, however, were far less common.

In fact, I don't think I'd ever seen a single one in the three years since we'd got the hovercraft. All we could do was approach the situation with great care and remember that it wasn't the same as your average rescue. At this point, with humans, we'd be shouting out to them:

We're coming alongside you.

Everything's going to be fine.

But there would be no use yelling at the horse and we didn't want it to get frightened to the point of hurting itself or someone else. As we let the hover down and climbed off, we immediately found ourselves in thick, boggy mud. It was going to be a bit of a task even getting to the horse.

We were definitely going to need our mud mats.

The mud mats were a vital piece of kit for us, thick pieces of rubber material with a strap attached so we could easily pull them out if they became submerged. They created a stable platform and a bigger surface area, so you didn't sink into the mud when you stepped on them. We created a path towards the horse, arriving by its side just as the girl was yanked out from her sitting position next to the animal. Although she was uninjured apart from a cut on her leg, she was understandably very upset.

'We need to get your cut looked at,' a rescuer was saying as we walked up to them.

'I've got to be here. I've got to stay,' she said, tears welling in her eyes.

My heart went out to her. I understood completely. If it was my black Labrador, Noah, in this situation, I wouldn't want to go either. But it *was* the right thing. I looked at Ian and tilted my head, suggesting that we speak to her first.

'Hello. I'm Emily from the RNLI,' I said gently. 'We're here to help now. You need to go and get some help, and we'll look after ...'

I suddenly realised I didn't know the horse's name.

'Bobby,' she said. 'I can't leave Bobby. I have to stay.'

Ian and I crouched alongside her.

'You can't, lovely,' I said. 'We need you to go and get your leg seen to.'

'And we're going to need lots of people to get Bobby out,' added Ian. 'So there won't be room.'

'But –' she started.

'Listen, it's really important for you to get to safety,' I said. 'But we'll do our absolute best for Bobby and we'll try everything we can to get him out.'

'OK,' she said reluctantly.

The man that had been digging her out earlier started taking her back up to the beach, with the assistance of one of the rescue team. With her clear of danger and just rescue crews remaining at the scene, we were now able to turn our attention to the horse.

Our very, very stuck horse.

I looked at it again in disbelief. How on earth were we going to do this?

Then, I looked at the team working around him and realised I recognised a few faces. It was some of the guys from my fire station, albeit from a different watch.

'Hi, are you all right?' I said.

'Yeah, excellent,' they said. They weren't fazed by anything.

Alongside them were the coastguard team, in their mud shoes.

If anyone could do this, I knew this lot could, so we got to work.

Between us, we formulated a plan. Despite it being a really unusual situation for him as well, Matt took control of coordinating and communicating between the different agencies we were working with, keeping everyone's safety front of mind. Our first course of action was to focus all of our efforts on trying to dig Bobby out of the horrible sticky mud. For an animal in such a predicament, he was remarkably calm, just standing there with his big, bemused eyes looking at us all.

I'm in quite the pickle, aren't I?

He was visibly shaken and was breathing really quickly, but he wasn't shuffling about or shaking his head. It sounds daft, but I think he knew we were there to help him. Seeing such a majestic animal so vulnerable and helpless made us even more determined. We couldn't use tools to dig around him, because of the risk of injuring him, so instead we got down on our knees and started digging with our hands. The mud felt thick and heavy as we clawed through it. I couldn't imagine what it would be like to be partially immersed in it.

He was leaning slightly more on his left side, which was where the coastguard team were digging, so Ian and I started working around a leg each on his right side, me at the front and Ian at the back.

'We need to try and dig him out as evenly as possible,' Ian said.

'Why is that?' I asked. I didn't doubt his experience, I just wanted to know what the risks were.

'Horses have really weak legs,' Ian explained. 'If we free one and he pulls up on that, or moves it in a funny direction, he could seriously injure himself.'

I knew that would have other consequences – for Bobby and for us – because moving a horse with an injured leg would be even more of a mammoth task. As we dug at pace, each focused on one leg, Ian was already thinking ahead to the next phase of the rescue.

'If he can feel his back legs are free, he should be able to start pulling out,' he said.

'We'll get you out, Bobby,' I said, trying to reassure him the best I could.

We dug and dug, trying to free him from the mud and give him some space to move. Every so often, Ian stopped and let one of the other crew take over so he could talk to Bobby. Clasping his hands together and filling them with fresh water that the crew had brought up, he cupped his hands to Bobby's mouth so he could take a drink from them.

95

As he drank, his breathing started to become more even.

Ian stroked his forehead and spoke gently to him. Although he couldn't move, Bobby had seemed nervous and twitchy, but as soon as Ian started chatting to him he seemed to settle.

'They can sense things,' he said. 'If you're scared of him, he'll know. If you seem nervous, he'll pick up on it and he'll react to it.'

Our initial nervous energy and adrenaline, working with such a big animal that we really didn't know anything about, had probably been rubbing off on him.

But Ian wasn't scared. He approached Bobby with real confidence. He had such affection for these animals after looking after his wife's horses for many years, and his calm voice seemed to soothe Bobby. Before long, Bobby seemed to really trust Ian.

And if Ian trusted us, that was good enough for Bobby.

He's like the horse whisperer, I thought.

His expertise was shining through, and I was so grateful to have him out with us. As time passed, we started to make some progress and unpack Bobby from the sludge around him. But with that progress came a risk for our crew and the other rescuers.

Once Bobby felt free enough, he'd start to move.

As soon as there was any sign of that, we had to move away immediately. An animal of his size bolting away could see him kicking a leg or trampling someone. That could easily end up in a serious injury.

Or worse …

It wouldn't be his fault, he'd just be acting on instinct. We had to understand that part of his nature and be vigilant, to make sure we all stayed safe.

96

As well as digging, we tried our mud lances to see if they helped to budge him. Sticking them into the mud around his back legs, we used them to inject water and compressed air into the ground, in the hope that it would soften the sand and create air pockets that would make it easier to free him.

'Be careful putting them in,' Ian warned. 'We still don't know where his legs are or where they are pointing.'

It was good advice. Horses legs could bend a few ways, and with them obscured by the mud we were working blind. As it happened, we also only had two lances when we really needed four – one for each leg. Plus, the mud he was stuck in was too thick for them to be effective anyway, so after a quick attempt we went back to digging by hand.

With every scoop his legs became more visible, and they eventually started to wriggle a little. As they did, Ian began pulling gently on the lead connected to Bobby's bridle, to try to encourage him out.

We all willed him on.

'Come on, Bobby,' I said.

The crew and other rescuers urged him on too. But it was a big ask. He was cold and tired, and he probably couldn't see anywhere that he'd be able to get a firmer footing. He was just surrounded by mud, mud and more mud. When he refused to move, we got back to digging. Sweat dripping from my forehead, I was reaching deeper and deeper. Then suddenly, Bobby started to move.

Really move, not just a wriggle this time.

'Stand back,' someone called.

Immediately we all moved back and watched, holding our breath collectively as he started to kick his legs around.

Inside my head I was screaming, *Go on, Bobby!!!*

He struggled valiantly, pulling forwards for a few seconds. Then, as suddenly as he started, he exhaled loudly and slipped back into the mud.

There was no time to waste. He'd done his best and now we had to get back to doing ours. Although he was by no means free, he was in a slightly better position, so we had to regroup and decide on our next steps.

'We just need to keep digging,' one of the rescuers said.

'Let's give him the room he needs,' I added.

While most of us got back to digging the claggy, wet mud from around him, the fire service guys prepared their mud mat, which was a lot longer than ours. The shore was about 300 metres away and the nearest patch of firm sand, suitable for a horse to stand on, was about 50 metres away. We were going to need something underneath his hooves to lead him along.

If we ever got him out.

We'd been digging for a good two hours and didn't seem to be getting anywhere fast. We weren't letting up, but the exhaustion was starting to creep in. Then, out of nowhere, Bobby tried to make a move again.

Instinctively we all moved back, gently encouraging him from the sidelines.

Come on, Bobby!

You can do it!

Go on, boy, pull!

He was giving it everything he had, straining hard to free

himself. Slowly the front of his body rose, revealing the tops of his front legs up to his ...

Elbows?

I hadn't had cause to think about naming the parts of a horse's body before, but his front legs were out up to the bend in the middle.

'Go on!' I cheered.

His hooves were out too!

Could he do it this time? *Could he?*

I knew we were asking so much of him. Still I willed him on. But Bobby was trying to push from his back legs. As he pushed, with nothing solid beneath his hooves, he was just sinking back in. After a few pained attempts, he collapsed with a wet thud and the sticky smack of mud against mud. As he sank again, so did my heart. We'd have happily waited all day for him to do things in his own time, but we didn't have that luxury.

The tide was on its way in.

Looking out towards the sea, I could tell we didn't have long.

An hour, tops.

As soon as it was in, we'd have to send the coastguard and fire crews to the shore. I didn't much fancy the chances of four of us moving Bobby. But if we couldn't get him out, he'd drown. I knew it and so did the other rescuers. As well as the increasing level of risk, we all had the promise we'd made to Bobby's owner weighing on us.

We'll do our best for Bobby. We'll get him out.

None of us wanted to go back and tell her we hadn't kept that promise. We couldn't let her down.

Or Bobby.

We had a responsibility to him too. By now he was standing tilted upwards with his front legs stuck out ahead of him, cold and tired, with a pleading expression on his face.

Please help me.

What were we going to do?

Things always changed on a shout, it was just how they worked. It might be the weather, the tide or the type of risk you were facing. When the situation changed, the plan had to as well.

I could tell everyone was feeling disheartened. Three hours in, it was no surprise. The mood changed and became more intense, as we all fought against tiredness and focused on formulating a Plan B that would save Bobby.

But we still had to consider what would happen if the tide came in.

Could we get some straps underneath him to help hoist him out?

What about attaching some flotation devices?

Could we swim him out?

In our hearts, we knew most of the ideas were impractical, if not impossible. If the tide *did* come in there would probably only be one option.

'We couldn't let him suffer like that,' Ian said. 'We'd have to, you know …'

He didn't want to say it and I didn't want to think it. But there was already a vet on the shore for that very reason.

We were racing against the tide and the most important tool in our armoury at this point was our effort. The main thing we could bring to the party was the willingness not to give up. We all knew we probably had one final attempt before the tide came in, so we threw everything at it, every piece of equipment and every last bit of energy we had. We pulled all of our mud mats around him, as close to his legs as we could get them and gathered together strops from the various rescue vehicles and vessels on the scene.

'Grab that strop,' someone called.

'Get the mat further under him,' said someone else.

Ian took Bobby's bridle and bit off and replaced it with a proper head collar, which was much more suited to pulling and controlling the horse. It looked like it was tricky to get on.

'You OK there?' I asked.

'The thing's caked in mud. I'm not sure it's on right, but it should do the trick,' he said.

As he finished securing the headgear, I dropped to my knees in front of Bobby with one of the other rescuers, and we started digging the mat further and further under the front of his body. Lifting his front legs up, I realised it was probably quite scary and uncomfortable for him, having all these humans in bright yellow suits and helmets surrounding him and rearranging his limbs.

'Sorry, mate,' I said. 'But we're trying to help you and we're doing our best.'

I took the little whinny he gave as an acknowledgement that he understood.

Do what you have to. Just get me out.

As we focused on making sure he had a firm footing in front of him, the rest of the crew worked on getting some big strops under his backside and tail. Because his position had shifted, we were able to get some under his middle too. If we could encourage him to move and use the strops to give him a hand, we might just get him out before the tide arrived.

Following Ian's example, we were all talking to Bobby now – reassuring words in calm tones that we hoped would make him trust us.

And work with us.

I think he knew we were building up to something, that time was running out, because he just sat there really calmly, like he was conserving his energy. Before we made our attempt, we huddled together.

'Everyone just grab a strop, and when he moves …' said Ian.

We all knew what we needed to do.

Pull as hard as we blooming well could.

We all took our positions, seven of us grabbing onto strops, sharing them and digging in, ready to pull for Bobby's life. Someone had hold of his headgear and started pulling on it gently to encourage him.

He knew it was time.

Slowly he came up onto his front hooves, then he started to move forward.

'Three, two, one … *pull!*' someone shouted.

I grabbed my strop and pulled with all my might.

For a moment there was tension, you could feel real movement, like we might actually be getting there. But then it all fell away. And so did Bobby.

'One of the strops slipped out of place!' someone shouted.

'Let's get them back in place,' Ian shouted. 'Try again!'

We raced back into position, making sure every single strop

was in the right place and well secured. Within minutes we were ready to try again.

This really is our last attempt, I thought.

'Three, two, one ... *pull!*' someone shouted, for a second time.

We all heaved, pulling and pulling and pulling, supporting every part of his body we could reach. Between grunts of effort, we called out his name.

'Come on, Bobby, you can do this!'

'Yes, Bobby, good boy!'

'Bobby!!!!'

All of a sudden his front was up. His middle followed and then, with a big, loud squelch, his back legs came free too. My heart was in my mouth as from the corner of my eye I spotted his powerful legs slipping around, but with one last mammoth pull from all of us he was up and standing securely on the mud mat.

'We've done it! Well done, Bobby!' someone shouted.

Thank goodness for that!

I think we were all a bit astonished to see the whole of Bobby just standing there in front of us – caked in mud but seemingly uninjured. In that moment I realised that Bobby wasn't actually that big a horse.

After hours and hours of digging and pulling it felt surreal. Our relief was palpable, but we couldn't celebrate just yet. We weren't quite done.

The tide was coming in fast and we had to get Bobby safely to shore.

Problem was, Bobby didn't want to move.

I'm standing here, and that's your lot.

Surrounded by miles and miles of the same mud he'd just escaped from, who could blame him? We tried everything to cajole him along the big mud mat. Encouraging words, pats on his hindquarters, gentle tugs on his headgear.

'What about these?' called one of the rescuers.

I looked over my shoulder to see him holding a big bunch of carrots.

Worth a try.

'Here you go, Bobby,' someone said.

One of us held a carrot just ahead of his nose, just out of munching distance, while we pulled him gently in our direction. The carrot certainly piqued his interest, that much you could see in his eyes. We let him take a bite, then moved away a bit further.

Bobby looked at the carrot. Then at us. Then he stamped his hooves a little on the mat. We knew exactly what that meant.

If you think I'm moving, you've got another thing coming.

He was a good horse, but, boy, was he stubborn. He just wouldn't budge.

The big pull and initial momentum meant we'd moved forward a bit, but we still had about 250 metres to the shore. With Bobby out of the mud, one of the crew had brought the vet from the shore to check him over. We turned to him for advice.

'How can we move him?' I asked.

'It's probably best to sedate him,' he said.

We couldn't have done this while he was in the mud because we needed Bobby to help us to help him at that point, but now it was different. The sedative would calm him down and reduce any distress he was feeling.

Then we can pull him back to shore, I thought.

All of the rescuers were on the same page. As the sedative did its job, Bobby would lie down and we could roll him onto the rescue sled the fire service team had brought. We moved the sled next to him and then the vet administered the sedative.

'It will take a few minutes to work,' he said.

So we waited.

And waited.

And waited.

Bobby was really still and his head dropped sleepily. You could tell the sedative was doing something. But he didn't lie down. After ten minutes we were still flanking him, waiting for him to go.

But absolutely nothing happened.

'Do you think it's worked?' I asked Ian.

'It's definitely worked,' said Ian. 'But it doesn't look like he's going down.'

Another five minutes passed. Bobby seemed sleepier and even started to lean into us. In fact, we were effectively holding him up and preventing him from falling.

But he still didn't lie down.

Another five minutes passed, then we called the vet back over.

Arms aching from holding the horse up with Ian, I addressed the vet.

'When's he going to lie down?' I asked.

'Oh, he might not,' he said.

My eyes widened in disbelief.

It would have been good to tell us that 25 minutes ago.

'And the sedative will be wearing off soon,' he added.

What the …?

There was no time to quibble over a misunderstanding. We had to find a way to move Bobby before the sedative wore off.

Or there'd be no chance of moving him.

There was only one thing we could think of. *He* might not be able to move.

But that didn't mean we couldn't move him …

Because he was still sedated, we knew he wouldn't panic, nor would he dig in and refuse to shift. A quick check with the vet confirmed that we still had a window of time left before the drugs wore off.

It might just work.

We gently nudged him onto the rescue sled, attached the fire service lines to the sled and hooked them up to one of the rescuer's vehicles. While we'd had our heads down in the mud, word about the rescue had spread locally. Once Bobby was out and people heard we were bringing him back to the beach, a crowd had started to gather. We needed to make sure that no one was too close when Bobby came round from the sedatives, as we didn't know how he might react, so a crew member went to the shore to clear the beach and disperse the onlookers, with the help of the police, who'd also arrived to assist.

Once the rescue sled was attached to the vehicle, one of the rescue crew jumped in the car, started the engine and began driving slowly and carefully towards the beach. We all flanked Bobby as we crept along the wet ground.

'Almost there, Bobby,' I soothed, as we drew closer to the remaining rescue teams.

I could see a horse box ready and waiting, brought down by Bobby's owners or someone from the horse yard. About halfway along we stopped to reposition our aching arms, ready for the final stretch of the rescue. Inch by inch the car pulled the rescue sled over the sand until finally, a few minutes later, we made it.

As we hit the sand of the beach, I exhaled a long, slow breath out.

We'd done it.

The noise of the sled transformed from a sloppy, dragging sound to a dry, scratchy one, and as it did, Bobby seemed to suddenly snap out of his sedated state. He looked around, gave a satisfied neigh …

And just walked off the sled!

My jaw almost hit the floor. I simply couldn't believe it.

'You couldn't have done that 100 metres back?' I exclaimed.

Maybe it was a coincidence, or maybe it was instinct and he knew that he was safe at last, but he simply trotted off, got straight into his horsebox and started chomping on his bale of hay. I looked around at the RNLI crew and the other rescue teams. They all looked as surprised as I was – even Ian. We all fell quiet for a moment, then we burst out laughing. It was as funny as it was frustrating.

Anyway, Bobby was back safely.

And that was all that mattered.

While he was taken away to be checked over, we went back to the place where he'd been stuck and started gathering all of our kit. Some of it was so covered in mud that we actually had to dig it up.

'We can't go back to the station without all the kit,' Ian said, 'or the coxswain will have something to say about it.'

It must have taken us a good 20 minutes to locate everything. We were exhausted from all the additional digging, but we were still pleased.

We'd told Bobby's owner that we would get him out.

And we did.

Through sheer determination, teamwork, a massive effort and the will to make good on a promise. It was a good day's work.

When we got the hovercraft back to the lifeboat station, it took us an hour and a half to wash it down and prepare it for the next service. Everything was caked in mud and the mess was absolutely unbelievable.

As we were finishing up, I messaged my husband, Pete.

'All done, be home soon,' I said.

'What was it this time?' he asked.

'A horse stuck in mud,' I replied.

'Oh right,' he said.

Oh right? I thought.

He was a firefighter too. Our jobs meant things that might sound dramatic to some couples just didn't to us. But *this*? This had been something unusual.

'No, you don't understand, we've been out here for more than four hours,' I said. 'I'll fill you in when I'm back.'

'Oh right, OK,' he replied. 'See you in a bit.'

A short while later I was home. I opened the front door and heard a familiar stampede of tiny feet.

My dog Noah and daughter Lily.

They both got so excited when I came home from a shout and it was always a race to get to me first. Today Noah was the winner.

Within seconds he was at my feet, wagging his tail and whining excitedly. He did the same thing every time, even if it was three in the morning.

'Hello boy,' I said, bending down to nuzzle him and give him a pet. As I did, he started sniffing at my hands and clothes.

'Are you wondering where I've been?' I asked, scratching around his ears.

He looked at me, head cocked in a slightly accusatory manner.

What animal have you been with today? It certainly wasn't me.

I must have smelled like a horse!

The next day we received word that Bobby was doing really well. A few days after that we received a thank-you letter from the young girl who Bobby belonged to. It was a lovely gesture and I was just pleased we'd been able to reunite them.

The rescue happened a few years ago now, but through Ian's connections we know that Bobby is still in a local stables. Apparently, he's had a few owners since the rider who got stuck in the mud with him, because little girls grow out of smaller horses quite quickly, but he's still going from strength to strength.

As RNLI crew we're trained to save lives at sea. I'm of the opinion that you should treat every life – whether it's a cat, a dog, a horse or a human being – with an equal amount of care. Each one deserves the same time and attention, and I know many of my crewmates agree. That belief certainly helped us keep digging and pulling to get Bobby out of his sticky situation!

WALRUS ON THE SLIPWAY

Phil John, Tenby,
March 2021

I was enjoying a weekend off when my phone beeped with a message from one of my deputies at Tenby Lifeboat Station. He ran a boat back and forth to Caldey Island, and it wasn't unusual for him to keep me up to date on what was going on out at sea and around the station, even when I was on leave. As RNLI crew, you were never really off duty.

But this time, when I opened the message, my jaw dropped in disbelief.

Phil. There's a walrus on the slip.

I looked up, blinked and looked down again. Had I just read that right?

Phil. There's a walrus on the slip.

A walrus!

I had. He was telling me there was a walrus on the slipway that we used to launch our lifeboat to emergencies. I mulled the gobsmacking information over in my mind.

We had seals and other maritime wildlife in Tenby. But a walrus?

I'd grown up in the town and served 28 years on the life-boats, as a volunteer for 16 years and as full-time coxswain since 2009. Never once had I seen a walrus out on the waves or on our beaches.

He had *to be taking the Michael,* I thought.

But why would he do that? I messaged back for confirmation.

A walrus? Are you sure? I typed.

Yes. A walrus, came the reply.

There was only one thing for it. I'd have to go down to the station to see for myself. On my way there I couldn't help thinking that it might still be a practical joke. If Jeremy Beadle were still around I'd have been expecting him to jump out at me with a camera crew.

Maybe it was just a very large seal?

But as the lifeboat station came into view I saw a huge grey lump, with two distinctive tusks and thick, wrinkled skin, stretched out in the sun at the end of the slipway.

Blooming heck!

It was – absolutely, definitely – a walrus. There was no mistaking that. When I entered the boathouse I found that the crew were as stunned as I was.

'He just turned up this morning,' someone said.

I headed out onto the slip and walked a little way down towards the creature. Not too close, though. I was aware that this was a wild animal – a rare one, in these parts at least – and we had no idea how to manage it. To my knowledge there was no module on 'removing a walrus from a slipway' in the RNLI training manual.

Why would there be? These creatures lived out in the North

The most decorated RNLI lifeboat crew member, Henry Blogg, with his trusty companion Monte.

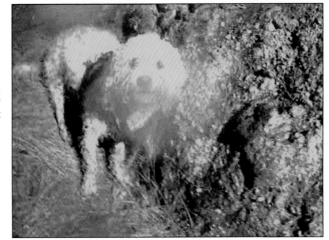

Bichon Frise Flossy trapped at the foot of dark cliffs at Porth Wen Bay in Anglesey.

Free at last!
Miracle the seal
safe and well after
her two-day ordeal
at Port Talbot.

Chiswick RNLI crew
member Mark Pusey
cradles soggy moggy Merlin
after a *Tom and Jerry*-style
rescue on the Thames.

RNLI lifeguard Scott Brierley improvises to rescue a distressed puffin
from the sea at Filey.

RNLI, coastguard, and Merseyside Fire and Rescue crews work together to free Bobby the horse from a sticky spot in Hoylake.

RNLI Tenby's surprise visitor basking on the slipway with his 'gull-friend'.

The ship's cat: seafaring feline Artie demonstrating water safety in his own lifejacket.

Ewe wouldn't believe it! RNLI Lough Swilly's crew rescue a Scottish Blackface sheep after a cliff fall.

Watch the birdie: Chris Walker from RNLI Tower poses for a selfie with Cleo, the rescued Harris's hawk.

RNLI Redcar crew member Ed Thomas cradling rescued pup Murphy,
while his own dog and search assistant Ollie stands guard;
(inset) Murphy trapped among recent rockfall near Huntcliff.

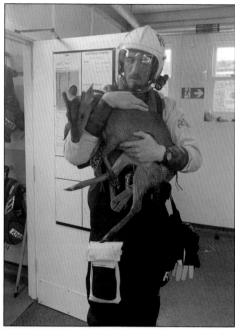

Ebbing the deer paddling furiously in the Solent (left) and his photo opportunity with RNLI crew member Myles Hussey at Cowes Lifeboat Station (right).

RNLI crew from Salcombe and Dart cutting whelk pots away from a 15-tonne humpback whale caught in lines at Blackpool Sands near Dartmouth.

Atlantic and the Arctic, and were rarely sighted in the UK and Ireland. If they ventured anywhere near, it would be hundreds of miles out to sea. Yet here we were.

One of the crew came out to join me. I knew they'd be looking to me for answers.

What do we do?

What if there's a shout?

How do we move him?

Truth is, I had no idea. What I did know was that if a shout came in now, our launch time would be delayed and that would put lives at risk. I brought my hand up to my mouth and tried to exhale the building tension.

'Ah Jesus, what do we do with him?' I said.

The crew member shrugged.

We were used to problem solving and coming up with answers quickly. But in this situation we were clueless. We had to change that, and fast.

The rest of the day passed in a flurry of calls, from myself and Phil Rees, our lifeboats operation manager, to our own line managers and all the way up the chain of command to head office in Poole.

Unsurprisingly, there was absolutely no precedent for our predicament, no policy written on how to deal with a walrus on your slipway. It just hadn't been seen before. Even the RSPCA, who were called upon to check on the welfare of the walrus, said it was the first time in the organisation's 200-year history they'd had such a request.

We were treading new ground, but it was a strange thing

to be leading the way on – and a dangerous one to boot. In the absence of any organisational protocols, I started searching for information on walruses and puzzled over our next move.

As we tried to come up with a plan, word of our unusual visitor spread like wildfire. We hadn't needed to put the news out there; you just couldn't miss the thing. All sorts of people had started to gather behind the lifeboat station on Castle Hill, from local families and tourists to the RSPCA and excited wildlife photographers.

It turned out that the walrus had first been spotted on Valentia Island in Ireland, before appearing in our waters. Somewhere along the way he'd been christened 'Wally' and the local press was following his movements.

With all eyes on the station, we couldn't afford to put a foot wrong.

We all completely understood the fuss. The station's communications team even shared in the excitement with a tweet jokingly lauding Wally as our newest 'recruit'. One of the privileges of living on the coast and working at sea was being part of an incredible ecosystem, with people and marine life living side by side as harmoniously as possible. If you took the operational headaches we were facing out of the equation, Wally was a joy to watch.

But if an emergency call came in, he'd hinder our ability to fulfil our responsibility.

Saving lives at sea.

The first question we had to answer was how could we get out to a drowning child or a sinking boat with a 600lb animal blocking our way? We did have another launch option.

'We could lower the boat out of the station into the water and launch from the RNLI mooring,' I suggested. 'But that would have to be a last resort.'

Our usual launch time was around 8 to 10 minutes. But with Wally in the way it would take us around 15 to 16 minutes, and we'd have nowhere near the same speed behind us setting off. Doing things that way would take us much, much longer.

When the RNLI was tasked to deal with animal incidents, I knew that some people viewed them as less important. But the purpose of any assistance to an animal was usually to protect human life. This was no different.

If we couldn't move Wally, those lost minutes could easily mean the difference between life and death for human casualties if we couldn't reach them in time.

So it was vital that we found a way to shift Wally.

But it wasn't just a case of doing whatever it took to move him. We had lots of other factors to consider. Wally was a protected species, so we had to respect that and find a solution that worked for both of us. We had to learn about the creature we were dealing with. He looked adorable enough, lolling about and snoozing away happily, but what if he was startled? In the absence of any formal guidance, I turned to the internet.

Disappearing down a rabbit hole of YouTube videos, I found footage of walruses just like Wally fighting with their own kind for territory and mauling polar bears as they protected their young. After a while I had to stop.

It brought home the level of risk my crew would face if we tried to move him.

117

As coxswain, it was my responsibility to ensure they always came home safe and well to their loved ones. The same was true in this situation.

Eventually, I stumbled across some useful information.

Walruses are affected by noise and disturbances.

Out in the wild, walruses lived in colonies of up to seven or eight thousand. A loud noise could spook them into a massive stampede, often resulting in their calves and smaller individuals being crushed. But since Wally was on his own and well away from the general public, that wouldn't be a problem for us.

Maybe this was something we could work with.

We consulted with the local RSPCA and got some additional guidance.

'Don't go down there unannounced,' they said. 'Set a siren off before you walk down the slip, so he knows you're coming.'

Apparently, walruses were also prone to heart attacks when frightened. It was good to know, as we certainly didn't want to harm him. Armed with as much information as we could find, we decided to give the loud-noise option a try.

We had a long metal pole in the boathouse and our slip was constructed from steel. The sound of metal on metal could make quite a racket, so it seemed like a good option. One of the crew was nominated to be noise-maker. As they approached the top of the slip, we took the RSPCA's advice on board and gave our siren a short, sharp blip.

Sure enough, Wally's big head tilted towards the sound.

The crew member took a few steps down the slip and Wally seemed to notice him but didn't seem alarmed. Next, the crew member took the pole and dragged it across the steelworks of the slip, as a way of 'shooing' him away.

A scraping, clanging sound rang through the air and the vibrations travelled along the tracks that Wally was flopped across. His head twisted quizzically again and then with a loud grunt he flipped onto his front and waddled a little, before dropping into the sea.

It worked!

'Well done!' I called to the crew member.

But three minutes later, he was back on the slip.

It was good to have a solution we knew worked in the bag, but it was still a big worry. Over the next few days the crew and I were in constant contact over the 'walrus situation'.

As the days and weeks passed we took note of Wally's natural movements. We realised that getting him off the slipway if a boat was coming back in wasn't a problem. As soon as he clocked us heading his way he'd flop into the water. Crowding out his vicinity with a boat seemed to naturally encourage him to move.

He wasn't always on the slipway, either. He tended to go off it on spring tides, heading off to sea for seven days or so at time, to feed. When he arrived in Tenby the RSPCA had been concerned he was a little underweight. Given the size of him, at first I found that surprising, but each time he came back from a fishing trip, he had a bit more weight on him.

Clearly eating well!

On the neap tides, which came about seven days after the spring tides, he'd be back for some rest. That was when we'd find him on the slipway.

The public seemed to be monitoring him as closely as we were, albeit for different reasons. We were lucky that there was no way to walk round to the slipway, or we would have had a real issue keeping people away. But people were still gathering behind the station or hiring boats to go out and take a closer look at him.

It was all very joyful. Shops in town went mad creating Wally-themed souvenirs, from mugs, cushions and T-shirts to drawings, postcards and even cakes. The local economy got a huge and welcome boost, with Wally merchandise flying off the shelves and tourists staying in hotels, eating in local restaurants and cafés. Some of the photography was stunning. My particular favourite was one of a seagull flying nonchalantly past Wally on the slip, taken by a local photographer called Gareth Davies. The caption was perfect.

Wally's got a gull-friend.

But still, he was a problem for us. We had challenges flying at us left, right and centre, and every move we made we were being watched, even when we were doing routine maintenance that kept our equipment fit for service. We'd found that power washing the slip sometimes had a similar effect to the metal pole. We followed a routine, giving the siren a little blip to let Wally know we were coming down to do some jobs and then just got on with it, never getting closer than about six to eight feet away from him.

Wally didn't like the power washer much, but it didn't do him any harm either, so it was a handy tool to use if we needed to launch. But sometimes, we just needed to wash the slip down and some people didn't like that.

One day I went down to hose the seaweed away. Wally was relaxing at the end of the slip, having acknowledged our now-customary siren blip. As I got to work, Wally was already stirring, the power washer his signal to scarper. I could hear a load of people shouting from the direction of Castle Hill. At first I didn't pay much attention, until I realised they were shouting at me.

'What are you doing?' one voice yelled.

'Leave him alone!' barked another.

'Can't you leave it for another day?' pleaded a third.

The answer was no. Seaweed or debris on the slip could cause all manner of problems when launching, meaning we'd take longer to get out and help people. I was all for accommodating Wally, because we didn't have much other choice, but the crew and I had to continue doing everything we normally did to keep the station fully operational. We were all as fond of Wally as the next person, and we weren't doing any of these things to be cruel or mean-spirited. It was always a matter of necessity.

Our 'blip and shoo' method worked for the first shout that came in while Wally was around. But the second one was at 2am in the pitch black and the fog. People thought he was just basking around in the daytime, but he was there at night too.

Coming from your bed in the middle of the night, with the added task of moving a walrus, wasn't a welcome addition to our routine. The call that had come in was a DSC distress, the radio equivalent of a verbal mayday. It was the kind of situation where every second counted. Our night vision was disrupted because we had to put all the big lights on to move Wally. It really put the pressure on. Thankfully, Wally quickly obliged and we made it out in as good a time as we could have hoped for in the circumstances.

But the more familiar Wally became with the various noises and techniques we used, the less inclined he was to budge.

He knew we were no real threat.

One day, when a shout came in, we tried the siren, the pole, the power washer and even a broom at close quarters, but Wally was simply not moving.

'What else have we got?' one crew member asked.

'Try the air horn,' someone suggested.

So we did. After a brief siren blip, a shore crew member edged down the slip with the air horn until he was a few feet away from Wally. Like every time one of my team was anywhere near him, I was on edge. Wally was aware he was there, but he wasn't ready for what came next.

Bwaaaaaaaaaaaaaaaaaaaaaaap!

It only took one blast and Wally was off.

I breathed a sigh of relief as the shore crew member got off the slip and the boat was able to launch.

The local media was covering every new method we used to move Wally, and from the outside it was all quite comical. But for me and the crew it was often frustrating and stressful.

For us the hesitation of a delay lasting even a few minutes was like being unable to move at traffic lights. At least that's how I explained it to my own family.

'It's like the traffic lights have gone green and there's cars behind you, but your engine's just stopped,' I told them. 'The frustration and the embarrassment building up, people urging you to go and you're thinking, *Come on, come on, come on*, and trying to get going, but you can't. That's what it feels like.'

Only the people urging us to move were people in distress at sea.

What looked like a bit of fun to the outside world was a serious business for us.

On 30 April, about a month after Wally had arrived in Tenby, our pagers went off. The coastguard was requesting we launch to reports of two canoeists that had got into difficulty between Stackpole and Broadhaven, about ten miles west of the town. It was the fifth shout we'd had with Wally at the station, and I was beginning to worry that he'd become a permanent feature.

Once again, Wally was reluctant to move and we had to deploy the airhorn. We got out to sea and located the casualties, who had managed to navigate themselves towards Stackpole Quays. We picked them up and took them the last half a mile into the quays, where the coastguard was waiting to recover them and check them over.

We were running back up the slip about 40 minutes after we'd launched.

It was a small, run-of-the-mill job and we'd got there in time to assist. But I couldn't help worrying.

How long would it be before we didn't?

Our call-outs were so varied. What if someone got cut off by the tide and we didn't reach them in time because Wally didn't move? What if we were too late to assist with a medical evacuation from a ship because we'd had to spend ten minutes blasting an airhorn? As the summer months approached, we'd only start getting busier and busier. What then?

It didn't even bear thinking about.

Every time Wally disappeared for a while, the general public was disappointed. But we were relieved. We needed him to go.

Maybe he knew he'd slightly outstayed his welcome, because sightings of him began to reduce, even further out at sea where he'd feed. Then one day, after three days without any sighting at all, he was spotted.

In Cornwall.

A gentleman from an organisation called Padstow Sealife Safaris had reported it to the local media in Padstow. Wally was about 70 nautical miles from Tenby, and with his top speed of about 21 miles per hour it was an easy swim.

Momentarily, I heaved a sigh of relief.

Thank goodness.

Then I realised. Padstow RNLI launched on a slipway, just like us.

They're in for a world of headaches, I thought.

We'd learned a great deal while Wally was with us and we knew it was stuff that wasn't in any official RNLI guidelines.

Not yet, at least.

I called down to the station to let them know what they might be in for and talk them through all the techniques we'd used.

'Noise is the best option, but he'll get used to it,' I warned.

'So have a few options?' they asked.

'Yes. And good luck,' I said.

I felt for them, but for all of our crew's sake and the people we might have to go out to help, I was glad. We could finally get back to normal.

Luckily for Padstow, Cornwall wasn't a prolonged stop on Wally's travels. A few days later he was spotted in Newquay at about 10 o'clock in the morning. I was in a regular meeting we have with the local council, but I made a mental note to call down with some advice once it was finished. But that didn't end up being necessary.

By lunchtime, Wally had already been spotted in waters near France.

I genuinely do hope Wally is off having a wonderful time on his adventures now, and I completely understand the way people reacted. It was an astonishing and unusual thing. Once in a lifetime? Maybe not. Throughout the whole thing, it struck me that Wally's arrival in Tenby was indicative of climate change in action. Both theories about how he'd got here supported that entirely. One was that he'd fallen asleep on an iceberg that had broken away and floated off, leaving him lost. The other was that he'd had to travel this far to find food.

I was so proud of the way the Tenby crew conducted itself under the immense pressure of doing their job in a way that worked both for us and for Wally. We're always happy to maintain that harmony between man and beast. Being part of a coastal community, we live alongside nature and respect it. But our overriding priority will always be to do everything we can to save lives and be there to help those who need us. No matter what the obstacle, we will always find a way.

8

ARTIE'S ADVENTURE

Rowena and Tim Heale,
Scarborough,
August 2020

It wasn't quite the journey we'd planned. My husband Tim and I loved to sail around Scandinavia and the Baltic, but because of the COVID-19 pandemic and quarantine regulations we'd decided to sail around home shores instead.

We'd set off from Gosport on 1 July and made our way along the south and west coast, through the Caledonian Canal and all the way to Inverness, anchoring as much as possible and only going ashore for water, food supplies or to wait for gales to abate. Other than that it was just our crew of three: Tim, myself and our two-year-old British Shorthaired cat, Artie.

That's right, our pet cat was on board with us for the entire trip.

It wasn't his first voyage. Artie got his sea legs very early, which had always been our intention. When we first went to meet the breeder just after Artie was born, we shared our plans with her.

'We sail a lot and want to take him with us,' I explained.

Fortunately, her son sailed as well, so she understood exactly what was needed.

'Oh, that will be great,' she said. 'If you get him used to being on board from the start, he'll be happy.'

We collected Artie from her when he was 16 weeks old. First of all we took him for a ride around in the car, to get him used to being in a moving vehicle. The following day we took him on board our boat *Talavera*, which was moored in Gosport, our hometown. We watched as this tiny, smoky-grey kitten fearlessly prowled around the deck and cockpit.

He wasn't fazed in the slightest.

The perfect ship's cat.

Over the course of a few weeks we alternated between driving him round in the car and taking him onboard the boat, then one day we took him out to sea. After that, we never looked back. Artie was part of the family and part of our crew. We didn't want to be without him.

We got him a pet passport, made sure he was fully inoculated and – as with any human member of the family – we took his water safety very seriously. Just like we practised 'man over-board' drills, we practised 'cat overboard' drills too. We had a fisherman's net on board in case we had to hoik him out of the sea, and from day one he even had his very own cat lifejacket.

We'd tested it out in the lounge at home first and it had been a bit tricky. The instructions on the pack said the jacket was for 'dogs and cats', but it didn't make sense. Dogs had long, straight backs, while cats arched theirs. It took us about ten minutes to squidge him into it, and when we finally had it secured he stood there for a moment looking at us, bewildered, and then, *donk,* he just keeled over on his side.

What the heck is this? he must have been thinking.

'You have to wear this so you're safe on the boat,' I explained, trying to coax him to step forward or backward.

But he wasn't having any of it. Every time we tried he just froze and plonked over on his side. I spoke to other seafaring cat owners who reassured me it was normal, though I couldn't help but wonder.

Am I being cruel? Should I give up?

But I knew it was important for Artie to be as safe as Tim and me at sea, so I made a few tweaks to the lifejacket so it wouldn't be so stiff on his back. I also made the reflective carrying handle more prominent and easier to catch with a boat hook if the need were to arise. He soon outgrew his first one and we weren't sure what size to buy, so we took him to the local agent for Baltic lifejackets at Hamble to try some on and find the perfect fit. The staff were really helpful and enjoyed watching Artie parade up and down in their showroom; he was – of course – a natural on the catwalk.

Artie very quickly got used to life on the waves. His cushioned carrier cage was wedged between the seat and the table below deck where he could happily snooze, or he could sit up in the cockpit, but his favourite spot was lying in his own home-made hammock close to one of the deck hatches, where he enjoyed sunbathing.

As we travelled around, he'd happily pose on deck in his lifejacket, nodding knowingly at other sea pets that we encountered and accepting tickles and treats from visitors. People absolutely adored him.

While Artie was confident on deck, he did have his moments. We had him on his lead one day, but had forgotten to put it on its extended setting. As he'd gone to leap down onto the pontoon, he'd gone *donk* mid-flight and plopped into the water. He wasn't impressed. Although he liked being *at* sea, being *in* it was another matter. Thankfully, our 'cat overboard' drills and his lifejacket meant we were well prepared, and we hooked him out to safety immediately.

It was a good lesson for Artie and for us.

He learned well. Most of the time when we were underway, he'd stay below deck. When he wanted to be sociable and sit with us in the cockpit, he'd wait patiently for us to put his life-jacket on. It was our one rule.

No lifejacket. No coming on deck.

We'd spent a week in Inverness, waiting for a weather window before we set off home to Gosport, intending to arrive home towards the end of August. We were getting a lot of easterlies and were waiting for a good northerly or westerly wind to get us all the way back down the east coast, about 620 miles. When the window of opportunity opened in the afternoon on 21 August, we put the sails up and got on our way, Artie safely in his carrier below deck.

The wind direction was right and everything was working in our favour, but having studied the weather forecast we knew not to expect a completely smooth journey. Sure enough, as we approached the North Yorkshire coast, things got really, really rough. We found ourselves in a confused sea, waves taller than our house towering above us. We considered going back, but we felt that turning the boat around in those conditions could be extremely dangerous.

Even more so than just carrying on.

Despite us both being experienced sailors and trusting the capabilities of our Hallberg-Rassy boat, it was at times frightening, yet also a challenging and exhilarating experience.

Ordinarily we'd do alternating watches throughout the night, one of us sleeping while the other stayed on deck. But as the boat was tossed up and down, side to side, over and over again, we decided to stay awake up in the cockpit together, grabbing a catnap here and there when we could.

All of our belongings were safely stowed and Artie was in his carrier, which was wedged securely in place, and already in his high-vis lifejacket. But that didn't stop us worrying.

After three days and nights we were exhausted, and sleep deprivation was really starting to set in.

Thankfully, though, before it could really take hold, the wind died down and the sea also calmed. We kept the main sail up and continued our passage with the assistance of the engine. By now we were about six or seven miles off the coast of Scarborough. There was no moon out, so we were sailing along in total darkness, Tim at the helm, when suddenly, *donk.*

The boat ground to a sudden halt.

'What's happened?' I said to Tim.

'I'm not sure at the moment but we've lost steering and we have no drive,' he replied. 'I think something might have taken the propellor off. I'll stop the engine to have a look – you grab a torch.'

Then we saw it. What looked like a big five-gallon oil drum, bobbing around at the boat's stern.

A lobster pot!

'It must have got caught around the prop and rudder,' said Tim.

Leaning over, we pulled and wiggled the pot, trying to free it, but it wasn't budging and it was too dark to really see what was going on down there. We stopped for a minute and scratched our heads.

What were we going to do?

Tim re-checked the radar, and then exasperation set in, as it had all been going so well up until that point.

'There's a commercial vessel approaching. Not imminently, as we are outside the shipping lane, but I'll let the coastguard know that we're having some trouble,' he said.

They'd know from our Automatic Identification Signal or 'AIS' that we'd stopped moving. We didn't quite know what help we might need, but we weren't going to be able to solve this alone. We also needed to make other vessels aware that we were here and immobile.

Tim grabbed the radio and called the coastguard. After giving our position, he explained our predicament. Not only were we without power or steering, but if we were to break free, we could be in serious danger of drifting uncontrollably into the shipping lane.

'We've picked up a lobster pot,' he explained. 'We're unsure what damage we may have incurred. The problem is below the water level and we're unable to safely reach it.'

'We'll send a lifeboat out,' the coastguard said. 'You'll need their powerful lights and they have specialist equipment. How many on board?'

'We're two persons and the ship's cat,' he said.

'The ship's cat?' the coastguard asked, just to confirm.

'Yes,' replied Tim.

Perhaps it was an unusual thing to hear, but given their line of work it was safe to say that nothing surprised them. They were always consummate professionals, even if something gave them reason to giggle.

As with everything, we treated Artie just like a person on board, even when dealing with the authorities.

'Has everyone got lifejackets on?' the coastguard continued, going through a list of standard checks.

'Yes, we both have,' Tim said. 'And the cat's got his own life-jacket too.'

'We'll get the lifeboat out to assess the situation,' the coast-guard said, immediately taking control.

The lifeboat was being sent from RNLI Scarborough. I popped my head below deck to check on Artie. Far from being scared or curious about what was going on, he was curled up in his carrier. It was past 10pm by now and he was enjoying a lovely snooze.

I'll leave him to it, I thought.

As we waited, both the RNLI crew and coastguard remained in contact with us. Despite being stuck out on the sea in the pitch dark, we had the reassuring sense of no longer feeling alone. In fact, the constant communication almost made us feel like they were already there.

The minutes passed and eventually we spotted lights in the distance.

'There they are,' I said to Tim.

An hour after we'd made the call, a great big Shannon-class all-weather lifeboat, with dazzling floodlights on, was alongside us. Relief washed over me as they brought the boat carefully alongside us and an RNLI volunteer crewman, in his iconic yellow kit, climbed aboard.

'Hi, I'm Paul Huggins,' he said, beaming warmly. 'What have we got here then?'

My mind was instantly put at ease, and I was sure that Tim's was too. We now knew we were in good, safe hands. With the water illuminated by the lifeboat's lights, it was much easier to see what was going on at the back of the boat.

'Looks like you might have caught more than one lobster pot there,' he said eventually. 'We'll get you sorted.'

After that, the RNLI took over. It was incredible watching them swing into action, knowing we'd just got them all out of bed at silly o'clock at night. Paul communicated with the crew, who moved the lifeboat to our stern and set about freeing our propellor. There was no yelling, just listening and calm conversation as they worked to find a solution to our problem. Everything was so professional and well rehearsed; it was an honour to watch.

As they worked, I offered my own bit of help.

'Would you like a cup of tea?' I asked.

'That would be lovely,' Paul said.

'Shaken, not stirred?' I joked.

As I handed him the cup, I noticed that he'd spotted Artie's carrier by the table, with the door open and Artie contentedly lying in his favourite sleeping position.

'So this is the ship's cat?' he asked.

'It is indeed,' I said. 'His name's Artie.'

'He looks happy enough down there,' he said, stirring his tea. But as he stirred in his sugar, a clinking noise rang out and I recognised the familiar scuffling sound below.

Moments later, a small smoky-grey head popped up in the now-busy cockpit, snub nose sniffing the air and big yellow eyes scanning around him.

Meow!

'Someone thinks he's getting fed,' chuckled Tim.

It was the middle of the night, but little Artie thought the clinking sound was his food being served. I could see him weighing up whether he wanted to venture out on deck.

He looked at me, then at Paul.

Meow, meow! came his indignant response.

He wasn't interested in joining us, he just wanted his food.

At the sound of the clink of the spoon on the cup, Artie opened one eye and examined the helmet- and lifejacket-clad stranger standing on *his* boat. But he didn't seem too perturbed; he simply yawned and fell back to sleep.

As the hours passed, it turned out Paul was right. There was a line running between a string of lobster pots. When we'd picked up the line it had completely encircled our rudder and locked itself around, keeping a second lobster pot down where we couldn't see or reach it. Even if we could have, it was in far too dangerous a position for us to attempt to free it ourselves.

A few of the crew owned sailboats themselves and were so considerate in their approach. We knew there was probably a quick and dirty way to solve the issue, but they were making every effort to ensure the boat wasn't damaged and communicated with us so we could make decisions together. Eventually, we had some success and the crew managed to cut away the pot that had been visible on the surface of the water.

'Give the engine a try now,' Paul said to Tim.

The engine fired into life.

'That's done it,' said Tim. 'The propellor seems to be free.'

'Great,' said Paul. 'Now we just need to get her in for a proper check-over.'

The crew advised that we go into South Bay, where we could safely drop anchor and they could bring the inshore lifeboat out with a diver, to get under the boat and have a proper look.

'I'll sort you something to eat now, Artie,' I said, tickling his head.

With that he gave another *meow* and darted back off below deck.

When we arrived at South Bay the inshore lifeboat was ready and waiting. The diver managed to cut the other pot free and there didn't seem to be any damage to the engine or propellor. Checking the forecast, we knew the weather was going to be changing the next day, so we decided to continue down with a stop at Grimsby.

We said our goodbyes to the RNLI crew.

'Thank you, Paul,' I said, before he climbed back aboard the inshore lifeboat. 'We really appreciate your help.'

'No problem at all,' he said. 'Take care.'

The rescue took about five and a half hours in total, after which the crew members could have just headed back home to their beds. Instead, they followed us for a few miles, just to be sure that our boat was fine and we didn't encounter any further problems. When we arrived in Grimsby a few hours later we spotted another boatful of RNLI crew. It was a common sight, and I was in the habit of always waving to the lifeboats anyway as a thank you for their work, but after the help they'd provided us I waved with extra enthusiasm.

I hadn't realised that they were waiting for us.

But they were.

The Scarborough crew had called down to Grimsby and asked them to make sure we arrived safely. It was lovely, humbling, and well above and beyond anything we could have asked of them. When we returned home to Gosport it was about four days after the rescue and two months since we'd first set off on our trip. We donated to RNLI Scarborough immediately and sent a note of thanks to the crew.

Sorry to have got you out of bed but, hey, cheers, guys. We really appreciate your help and genuine attitude to helping those in need. From our hearts, and Artie the ship's cat, we thank you.

While we've always understood that the RNLI are there to help and save lives at sea, I'm not sure I understood how equally they treat our furry and feathered friends. As a pet owner at sea, it just gives you even further peace of mind. You obviously have to do your bit, as we do with Artie, but if you need them, they will be there. Paul and his RNLI colleagues were so respectful of Artie and absolutely treated him as a member of our crew – even if Artie did snooze for most of the rescue!

(9)

SHEEP DRAMA AT LOUGH SWILLY

John McCarter, Lough Swilly,
August 2016

Being part of the RNLI wasn't always about going out on a shout. As an organisation almost wholly funded by donations, fundraising was a vital part of our job too. After all, if we didn't have the funds, how would we keep the boats in the water and continue our service?

In the summer months the RNLI Lough Swilly team would often take advantage of the pleasant weather and people's fascination with our jobs and boats by hosting fundraising days with the crew, bringing along vessels for members of the public to explore.

It was a sunny Sunday in August 2016 and we'd taken our Shannon-class all-weather lifeboat up to the quays in Ramelton, a town at the other end of the lough to our station. The Shannon craft, named the *Derek Bullivant*, was still new to the area and causing quite a stir. Sixteen months earlier, RNLI Lough Swilly had the honour of being the first station in Ireland to receive one. It was as exciting for the crew as it was for the public, not least because the designer of the boat was a gentleman called Peter Eyre, who had been rescued by a Lough Swilly lifeboat when he was 14.

In its first year of service the boat had seen 19 shouts.

As soon as we were tied up at the quay, people had poured onto the vessel, marvelling at the boat as a feat of engineering and asking the crew all kinds of questions. The community in Ramelton had always been incredibly supportive of us, so it was a real pleasure to see them enjoying the boat and be able to share stories with them.

While we were away, our inshore lifeboat – an Atlantic 85 – remained at the station, ready to launch if requested. Fundraising might have been a vital part of our role, but emergencies didn't stop for lifeboat days, so we made sure there was always a crew and boat available in case the pagers went off.

We'd been at the fundraising day for a few hours and I was speaking to some visitors when my phone rang. I glanced down. It was Malin Head Coast Guard.

'Excuse me one moment,' I said, stepping away to a quieter spot.

I was the lifeboat operations manager at Lough Swilly and we operated one of the largest areas of water in the whole of Ireland and the UK, covering a 27-mile-long inshore lough and all the way out into the North Atlantic. Our nearest stations were Arranmore, about 70 miles west along the coast, and Portrush in Northern Ireland, about 50 miles in the other direction. It was a huge area, with a reputation for being rough and rugged, and I looked after all the station and lifeboat operations in Lough Swilly. If something was happening involving our crew, boats or station, I was fully responsible for it.

In layman's terms, the buck stopped here.

'Hello?' I answered.

'Hi, John, we need you down at the other end of the lough,' the coastguard said. 'There isn't life at risk as yet. But there's a sheep in bother.'

A what, now?

'Pardon?' I replied.

'There's a sheep in bother,' he repeated.

I stifled a laugh. 'Yeah, you're having me on.'

We were used to varied shouts, from pleasure crafts in difficulty to big commercial shipping jobs, but while the area was very agricultural, we rarely got tasked with animal rescues. When they came along, it was always a surprise.

'No, no, I'm not,' the coastguard continued.

I listened as he explained how some local fishermen had spotted the animal stuck on a ledge in a ravine at Leenan Head. The sheep wasn't so much of an immediate problem as the farmer, who didn't want to lose one of his prime stock. He and his family were at the top of the cliff, and looked as though they might try to retrieve it themselves. When that happened, it usually ended up with the person – or persons – in more trouble than the animal.

We couldn't have that.

I thought for a moment. I knew the stretch of cliffs well and it was navigable by boat, but the Shannon, currently in Ramelton, was too far away. The Atlantic 85 was closer and better suited to the job.

'We're up in Ramelton with the all-weather, but we'll launch the ILB,' I said. 'It'll be able to get into that area you're talking about a lot more easily.'

I paged the crew immediately, and minutes later they launched.

Once they were on their way I got on the radio of the Shannon and spoke to the helm, Eamonn Mahon. An unusual job was always good for the crew, and I couldn't think of any time these four lads on the boat had been called out to an animal. Over the years we'd had to coax some lost cows and bullocks back into the shallows, and on very rare occasions we'd retrieve a dog that had got itself stuck while its owners walked it along one of our beaches, but animal shouts really were few and far between, so I shared some advice.

'This rescue will be really exciting, but once you've got the sheep you'll need to concentrate on keeping him still and quiet until you get him back to shore,' I said.

Sheep were skittish creatures at the best of times and they were big too. The last thing you wanted was one kicking and panicking in your lifeboat. It was dangerous for the crew as well as for the animal.

'OK,' Eamonn said.

'Let me know when you're out there,' I said.

Thankfully, when they arrived at the scene the weather wasn't causing any problems. Approaching those cliffs in a big swell could be treacherous, but it was sunny and calm. Even more importantly, they could see the farmer and his folks were at the top of the cliff, staying put. The sight of them put the reason for the shout into perspective

If any of them had even tried to go down the cliff, sure as fate they would fall and end up hurt. While the buzz of the fundraising day continued around me, I listened in over the radio as the crew communicated with the coastguard. I'd been with the RNLI for 11 years, but only in charge for four. However, I'd lived on Lough Swilly for more than 40 years and was a regular keen sailor, so I knew the coastline well. I could picture the scene clear as day.

The cliffs were about 300 feet high. From what I'd been told, it seemed like the sheep had gone on a little walk down them but lost its footing and slipped about 50 to 60 feet, finding itself on a ledge just above the water level. A sheep is a fairly sure-footed creature and getting down cliffsides is in its nature. But getting back up them could be another matter altogether, especially if it couldn't see a clear route back. I imagined it was also a heck of a lot more daunting. To put it in a human context, it was like walking across a gaping ravine on a little rope bridge, then turning round and realising you had to go all the way back.

Terrifying.

The fishing boat that raised the alarm was still at Leenan Head, along with a kayaker. They pointed the sheep out to the lifeboat crew, and the flat, calm conditions meant the crew were able to get right up to the ledge.

'We've tried to shoo it back up the cliff,' Eamonn reported. 'But it's not budging. Poor thing is shaking.'

'You're going to have to grab hold of it,' I said into the radio. 'Just try not to get it in the water.'

It turned out the sheep was an adult Scottish Blackface, a hardy breed that on average weighed about 145lbs.

Heavier than a barrel of beer!

But if its fleece got wet, that weight would increase significantly – and if it entered the water … well, they might lose it altogether. None of us wanted that. The first phase of the rescue seemed to go successfully. One of the crew and the kayaker had entered the water, approached the ledge and somehow managed to gently manoeuvre the sheep into the kayak.

All well and good, but now they had to get it into the lifeboat.

One of the crew, Seamus McDaid, had been assigned as sheep-grabber. He was positioned at the bow of the boat and was awaiting instruction. He had farmers in his family, but had never worked on a farm; in fact, he was a fashion retailer by trade. Nevertheless, he'd seen working farms, so there was a chance he'd be able to draw on some of that experience.

'He's approaching him carefully,' Eamonn said from the helm. 'Trying to keep him calm.'

'Great,' I said. 'When he gets it, tell him to keep a tight hold.'

For a while the radio went quiet, then it crackled back to life.

'OK,' said Eamonn, stifling what sounded like a laugh. 'He's got hold of it by its fleece.'

I could hear a bit of background noise.

The sound of a struggle? I wondered.

Turns out, the sheep wasn't coming easy. It wasn't a tense struggle. More a source of hilarity as Seamus tried to get the animal in his grip. He had made a few lunges but the sheep had leapt out of the way. Now that he had hold of him and had got him onto the bow, he wasn't quite sure what to do.

'He's keeping tight hold of him,' Eamonn reassured me.

Truth be told, there wasn't much more he could do.

'Tell him to think of a sheep being sheared,' I said. 'Turn it on its back and hold it between his legs.'

Sheep have a notoriously hard time getting up off their backs. But if they let it get upright on its legs, it'd be off out of the boat and back in danger. Seamus just needed to get it on its back and hold tight. The radio went quiet again as Eamonn relayed my message.

By now, other crew members who were up at Ramelton with me had gathered around, amused and intrigued by what was going on.

And offering their advice too, of course.

Messages pinged back and forth on the radio as the crew struggled to get the bemused sheep fully into the lifeboat. As the tension grew, the volume of our exclamations crept up as well. It sounded like they'd almost cracked it.

'It's on the boat!' Eamonn reported.

'Get it between your legs!' I shouted instinctively.

Suddenly, I snapped back into my surroundings. A couple of visitors who were passing by us on the Shannon stopped dead in their tracks and stared at me, jaws wide open. There I was, a lifeboat LOM, sitting at the radio – a place most people consider a spot where serious work takes place.

Shouting, 'Get it between your legs.'

What must it have sounded like?

I smiled at them reassuringly.

'We're assisting in the rescue of a sheep up the coast.'

Remarkably, they believed me. I wasn't sure I would have without further proof, but they went on their way. As they did, I thought it was actually quite a nice thing for them to have witnessed. It showed we were never off duty.

Not to mention the breadth of our work!

I turned my attention back to the radio. It seemed like the advice worked. Seamus had the sheep on its back, with his own legs locked around it.

'We're heading to meet its owners and hand him back now,' Eamonn said.

'Good work,' I said. 'Well done!'

The crew had managed the whole situation brilliantly and proved there really was no job too difficult or unusual for us to tackle. The harbour they'd arranged to drop the sheep off at was only five or ten minutes away. The sea was still calm and the boat wasn't likely to bounce around much, but I could guarantee that it would have felt like the longest journey of Seamus's life.

A few minutes later the crew radioed to say that the sheep was safe and well, and had been reunited with its very happy owner.

'How's Seamus?' I asked.

'Oh, you know ...' Eamonn said, before dissolving into laughter.

Jokes aside, I was really proud of them. Yes, they'd had an enjoyable service, one they'd probably talk about for years. But they also realised the value of it. If they hadn't got out there, the sheep could have been seriously hurt or some of those folks would have tried to get it back up the hill themselves. The story could have had a tragic ending.

Thankfully, it didn't.

By the time we returned from Ramelton, the crew were already back and had prepared the Atlantic 85 for its next service. The boat had needed a serious clean down after the shout, to get rid of the dirt and fleece. In the days that passed, the escapade was the talk of the station and poor Seamus the target for all sorts of light-hearted ragging about his newfound sheep-wrangling skills.

Hey, Seamus, you could go out and catch your own wool for the shop now.

He took it in the spirit in which it was meant, of course.

The rescue wasn't just the talk of the boathouse either. Perhaps it had happened on a slow news day, because the following week all the local papers reported on the dramatic sheep rescue that had taken place at Leenan Head.

The story lost nothing in the telling.

But by early September – much to Seamus's relief – the attention seemed to die down. That is until a local society for breeders and farmers of the breed of sheep we'd rescued got in touch.

'We were delighted with what you did,' the woman on the phone said. 'You got the sheep back and most importantly made sure none of our farmers were injured.'

'The crew were just doing their job,' I said.

'We're going to sell some sheep to raise money for the RNLI at the first sheep mart next year in Raphoe,' she said. 'We'd love you to come and tell us more about what you do.'

151

It was a lovely offer, so of course we accepted.

It was a cold, dark February evening when the day of the first sheep mart of the year took place in Raphoe. Along with Eunan McConnell, one of our deputy launching authorities, I made the drive inland to the town for a 7pm start.

Despite having a wee bit of experience of farmers' markets, I still found the whole environment a little alien. The place was buzzing with farmers when we arrived and the lady who ran the society was there to meet us.

'Come and have a cup of tea,' she said, leading us to the café. 'Then I'll take you to the ring.'

After a quick brew, the auction was about to start.

She ushered us through all kinds of pens and then gestured to a door.

'That way,' she said.

I pushed the door open and we stepped forward.

What have we let ourselves in for? I thought.

We were standing in the middle of the sale ring, with about 150 farmers staring back at us. The man from the sheep mart got proceedings underway.

'We'll be starting shortly, but first of all John McCarter, lifeboat operations manager of the RNLI, is here. He's going to talk to you about the work of the RNLI before we sell the sheep.'

Then he turned to me.

'John,' he said, gesturing to me to take the stage.

I swallowed hard. I thought we might be talking to a smaller crowd, or going around chatting to people in small groups.

I hadn't realised I was going on public display.

I glanced at Eunan, wondering if he preferred to do the talking bit.

'They asked for you,' he said, shrinking away.

I'd seen some daunting sights in my time, but looking up at all these farmers who were eyeing us up as if we were stock for sale was on a whole new level. Raphoe was much further inland, so this wasn't an audience that would have much prior knowledge of the RNLI, so I started to explain about the work of the RNLI, where we're located and how we operate, before relaying the story of our Scottish Blackface friend. A few minutes in, I mentioned that the service received no financial government support or other funding.

Every single one of them looked stunned.

It was the same everywhere. No matter how many places I went to speak about the RNLI, no matter how many individuals I spoke to, they never fully understood just how important donations were to keep this emergency service running.

'We couldn't do what we do without the generosity of the public,' I concluded.

It seemed to go down well, and we received a burst of applause. Then the three sheep that were up for sale to raise money for the RNLI were brought into the ring. Eunan and I moved quickly out of the way.

'We don't want to end up getting sold ourselves,' I said.

Stepping out of the ring and moving to the sides, we watched as the auction sprang to life, with farmers bidding over one another.

'One hundred euros!'

'Two hundred euros!'

'Three hundred euros!'

Before long all three sheep had been sold, and it seemed that my talk had done the trick. The price of the sheep had clearly been pushed up on the basis of the rescue we'd undertaken and the discovery that we relied on donations. After the bids were tallied up, the lady from the society appeared again, this time with a signed cheque.

'There you go,' she said. 'And thank you again for what you did.'

I looked at the cheque and showed it to Eunan. A grand total of €1,000 had been raised for the RNLI – almost double what would usually be made from a similar lot.

'I don't think we would have made as much auctioning us off,' I joked.

It was absolutely wonderful, a lovely gesture.

And definitely worth Seamus wrestling the sheep.

Whether it's humans or animals we're rescuing, being part of the RNLI is very special. You're there to save lives – and livestock in this case. Notwithstanding the very serious job we do – and this area has seen plenty of maritime tragedy – we have a great time together and experience some really unusual and exciting jobs. It's a pleasure to do it. And it's very rewarding, particularly when you see local families whose lives might have been different if RNLI volunteers hadn't been there.

Animal rescues around Lough Swilly remain rare. In fact, I don't think we've had a significant one since the sheep. The RNLI's official retirement age is 70 and I'm about two years off that now, but they seem to be relaxing the rules a little, so maybe I'll still have time to see a few more!

TRACKED BACK TO TOWER

Steve Doherty, Tower,
February 2019

I was working the day shift at RNLI Tower with three other crew members when the phone rang. Unlike other lifeboat stations, Tower was crewed 24 hours a day and we operated in 12-hour shifts. This was absolutely vital, given that we were the busiest station in the country, serving a stretch of the Thames that was always active.

The call was from an off-duty member of the crew. He'd been out on a walk along the river and spotted something unusual in the water.

'He reckons there's an eagle in distress in the river,' my crewmate Steve King said.

'An eagle?' I asked.

Were they even native to the UK?

Steve shrugged. If they were, they certainly weren't exactly a common sight in London. We contacted the coastguard, who gave us the go-ahead to launch. Based on the description we had, it seemed to be some kind of bird of prey, which meant there probably wasn't a pet owner at risk of leaping in after it.

In fact, most people wouldn't even spot a bird caught in the river's tides.

But there was still always a chance.

With a second crew and boat at the station ready to go if another shout came in, we were able to quickly launch and make our way a few minutes up the river to the spot near Embankment Pier where the bird had been seen.

It was a strange sensation, going out on a shout to such an unusual animal. I'd been at Tower for a year, after moving to the city to join the London Ambulance Service. I'd been a volunteer since I was 17, first in my hometown of Lough Swilly in County Donegal, then in Cowes on the Isle of Wight.

In that whole time, I'd only once been tasked to an animal – a dog.

Nothing as exotic as an eagle!

Powering out towards Embankment Pier, with Steve, Chris Walker – another crew member – and our commander Craig Burn, I wondered how we were going to tackle the shout. The RNLI provided animal-rescue training, and there were operating procedures for everything from cats to cows. But there was no standard procedure for a bird. It was going to be a case of adapting our animal training to the situation, and protection would be important.

Heavy-duty gloves on.

Visors down.

As we approached Embankment Pier we saw some pedestrians waving at us and pointing to a spot in the water. Sure enough there was a bird in the water, flapping about frantically. As we moved nearer, the pedestrians gave us some additional information.

'It landed on one of the railings and then fell into the river,' one said.

'It's been struggling to get itself out,' said another.

I looked over at the bird again. It really was a sorry sight. On closer inspection, it was smaller than I'd expected and it didn't look like an eagle. Whatever it was, its feathers certainly weren't designed to be in the water. They'd become waterlogged and heavy, and were weighing it down. Add the chop and flow of the river to that, and it was in a real predicament.

It simply wasn't strong enough to pull itself out.

'We're just going to have to grab it and get it in the boat,' Craig said.

As we came alongside the bird, Steve and I positioned ourselves on the side of the boat, ready to scoop it up. Steve had a navy-blue RNLI blanket on hand too, ready to wrap the bird in.

For warmth and to stop it flapping around.

As we waited for the right moment, I noticed the bird wasn't making a sound. I'd expected it to be squawky and loud, but it was just silently flapping its wings and stretching its head skywards, trying to keep its beak above water.

I looked at Steve and nodded.

'One, two, three ...' I counted.

Then, taking a side each, we grabbed the bird's body and lifted it out of the water. Once it was in our grasp, Steve grabbed the blanket and wrapped it swiftly around the bird.

'The poor thing's freezing,' he said.

Maybe it was exhausted, maybe it was the blanket restricting its movement, or maybe it just knew we weren't there to harm it, but as soon as it was in the boat, it stopped thrashing around. It was around 40 to 50 centimetres long, with a yellow beak and big, beady, yellow-ringed eyes. It definitely wasn't an eagle.

So what was it?

A quick Google search on one of the lads' mobile phones suggested it was a female Harris's hawk, based on its size and markings. But even knowing what species it was, we were still stumped – what did we do with it now?

After allowing the bird to warm up and dry off for a few minutes in the blanket, we decided to unwrap her and check if she was injured. If she wasn't, we assumed she might just fly off, although our new friend didn't seem keen to leave us.

Once she was out of the blanket, she gave her wings a little shake, then just perched on the side of the lifeboat, looking around at us all. It was such a bizarre situation – we were sure no one would believe us, so we took a quick selfie with the bird.

For posterity, of course.

The bird didn't flinch. In fact, she posed perfectly with us.

'Does she have a tag or anything?' Craig asked.

Steve and I looked at her feet. Around one of her legs was a ring, with numbers punched into it.

'Might be an ID code?' I suggested.

'Or a phone number?' said Steve.

Whatever it was, we needed to return to the station to further investigate. The bird didn't seem injured, but she wasn't moving anywhere either.

'We're going to have to take her back with us,' I said.

As we wrapped her back up in the blanket, to keep her and the crew safe, Craig got us underway back to the station. Once she was safely out of the boat we took her to the medical room in the boathouse. We didn't have a cage or anything to hand, but once we'd freed her again from the blanket she was very calm, so we popped her down and stepped away, waiting to see how she'd respond to being indoors. We decided to keep a couple of crew members with her at all times, and while we watched her the others hopped on the computers to try to figure out where she'd come from and who she might belong to.

Usually when we had a casualty in that room, we'd be talking to them and reassuring them, or medics would be attending to them. If it was a dog, we might pet it and comfort it, but in this scenario we had no clue. All we could do was watch. As we looked at her, she just stared back. After a while, we noticed her starting to wilt a little. The room was warm and this seemed to be affecting her.

'Let's take her into the mess room, it's cooler,' I said.

'Good idea,' said Steve.

She perked up immediately. The mess room was the area where we'd eat together or grab a cup of tea, and having a hawk knocking around added to the surreal nature of the day. She seemed quite tame and was never aggressive, appearing just grateful to have been rescued and to be somewhere that wasn't cold and wet.

She must have an owner, I thought.

She was so comfortable around us. So comfortable, in fact, that while Steve was sitting in the mess-room armchair, she hopped over and sat on his arm. For the next couple of hours she sat there, looking around and taking in the sights and sounds as the crew tried to get to the bottom of where she'd come from.

And what the heck to do with her …

They were reaching dead ends all over the place. The RSPCA and London Zoo had no records of anyone missing a hawk, and because she wasn't injured the RSPCA couldn't take her in. Even the local council couldn't help.

We were running out of options.

'We might have to pass her to the zoo to look after,' someone said.

As we considered our options, the bird's manner suddenly shifted. She started to move around, agitated, as if her senses had been heightened by something. We looked around, puzzled. It wasn't like someone had moved suddenly, or made a loud noise. So what was happening?

Nothing had changed.

Not that we'd noticed, anyway.

As she shifted, her head started looking around intently, turning 180 degrees in one movement, and then suddenly …

Whoosh.

She opened her wings wide.

'Woah!' I gasped, as we all instinctively stepped back.

They must have been over a metre long tip to tip. With the cream-and-brown plumage on the underside of her wings magnificently displayed, she was quite a sight to behold and looked much more powerful than the bedraggled, exhausted creature we'd fished out of the Thames. What *was* she up to?

And why now, two and a half hours after the rescue?

'Maybe she wants to fly away?' I suggested, scratching my head.

It was plausible that she'd just needed a bit of time to recuperate after her ordeal. Maybe this was her way of telling us she was ready to go.

'Let's get her outside,' someone said.

Letting her hop onto the gloved arm of one of the crew members, we took her outside and placed her on a rail.

'Off you go,' I said.

But she just sat there, looking at me blankly.

Had she only wanted some fresh air?

We waited for a few minutes, but when she showed no intention of flying off, we brought her back into the mess room, where she returned to sit on Steve's arm. Almost at the same moment as she settled, the gate to the station buzzed.

We all froze for a moment, wondering if the noise would set her off again, but she just sat there calmly. I shrugged, still completely baffled.

'I'll go and answer it,' I said, heading outside.

As I opened the gate, the man standing in front of it with his back to me turned around. He was wearing what looked like a large glove or gauntlet on one arm, and there was a look of concern on his face.

'Hello,' I said.

'Hello,' he replied. 'Have you … have you got a bird in there by any chance?'

I felt a smile slowly spreading across my face.

'Funnily enough we do,' I replied. 'A hawk.'

You could see the relief wash over him immediately.

'Oh, thank goodness,' he said. 'I tracked her to the bridge, but I couldn't see her. Then I saw the station.'

'You tracked her?' I asked.

'Yes, she's fitted with a tracker and I can see where she is on my app,' he explained, showing me his phone.

'Incredible,' I said. 'Come on in.'

The man followed me into the mess room. As soon as he stepped in, the bird's head turned towards him and she started flapping her wings excitedly.

'Cleo!' he exclaimed.

The bird spread its wings again and glided a short distance across the room to land on the man's gauntlet.

'Looks like we've found your owner then,' someone chuckled.

As the pair were reunited, we pieced together the rest of Cleo's story. Her owner explained how they'd been tasked with chasing away the pigeons on the Embankment. She'd been hard at work when another bird of prey had appeared, a kestrel. Although much smaller, it had attacked Cleo and spooked her. The owner had seen her dart off, but he had no idea where she'd gone. In the meantime, as she'd made her escape, Cleo's tether, a thin leather strap that was used to keep control of her, had got tangled around her and she'd fallen into the water. The owner hadn't seen that happen, though, so using the tracker – which was in the ring on the bird's leg – he'd followed her location on the app to the bridge near the station.

After he'd explained things from his side, we filled in the gaps for him, explaining how we'd been alerted and had scooped her out of the Thames.

'She seems unhurt,' I said. 'And she's been really well behaved.'

'She did seem a bit agitated a few minutes ago, though,' Steve added. 'Her head was spinning and she spread her wings out.'

'Ah,' the owner said, 'I was blowing her whistle.'

Turns out he had a special whistle to call her back. He'd reached the bridge by the station and started blowing it, thinking she might be stuck underneath. She could hear it, but we couldn't.

'Well, that explains that then,' I said.

'Thank you so much for helping her,' the man said. 'I really appreciate it.'

'No problem at all,' I replied.

As he turned to leave, we said our goodbyes to our unusual visitor.

Bye, Cleo!

It was a lovely thing to witness the two reunited. The station did feel a bit empty without Cleo's beady eyes on us for a while, but we were soon back to work. Despite it being a great story, I don't think any of us fancied having a bird back in the boathouse any time soon.

It was certainly a strange shout, but remarkably not the most unusual I've ever been tasked with. That dubious accolade goes to a call from a member of the public who reported what they believed to be a large life raft drifting away down the river.

When we got there, it was a 25-foot inflatable banana!

Being crew with the RNLI is an honour and a huge responsibility. We approach every shout with the same attitude and take our duty to the public very seriously. We see successes and some far sadder outcomes. Between those we get these quirky incidents, which add to the variety of our work and bring a bit of lightness to some of the darker and more difficult moments!

11

THE HUNT FOR MURPHY

Ed Thomas, Redcar,
April 2021

It had been an exhausting evening for all of us, but especially for the lifeboat crew, who had been out on a search for a man who'd gone missing while out walking his dog. As I washed down our Atlantic 85 lifeboat, the *Leicester Challenge III*, after the shout, to ensure she was ready for her next service, I reflected on the events of the evening. I was pleased the shout had been a successful one and that the crew was back safely, but it all felt quite bittersweet.

In my mind at least, the job wasn't quite finished.

Our pagers had gone off at 10.06pm on Friday, 9 April. An immediate launch of our lifeboat had been requested to assist the coastguard, police and members of the community who'd already been looking for the missing person – a local man named Mike – since mid-afternoon.

They'd searched everywhere they could reach, from the town centre to the nearby beaches, and had even used mobile phone triangulation to try to locate him. When they'd exhausted all those options there was only one place left to look.

Huntcliff.

It was a dangerous stretch, with cliffs towering hundreds of feet over the piles of rocks that had tumbled down from them over the centuries. Some were smooth and sea-worn, having been there for many years. Others were jagged and sharp, with the piles of smaller, lighter-grey rocks sloping gradually down from the cliffs – a clear indication of a more recent rockfall. When the tide was out you could walk around the cliffs, but when it came back in it was easy to find yourself trapped, particularly at the point not far from Saltburn, known as the 'cut-off'. If you were past that point when the tide came in, there was no way back.

For lifeboat crew the whole area was a place of trepidation. A call to those cliffs was often undertaken to recover a body and every job there was fraught with risk. Other members of the crew had been on shouts under the cliffs where the lifeboats had been damaged by being pounded by the surf into the rock, and I'd almost been hit by a falling rock myself once while responding to a call for help. Needless to say, none of the crew were particularly fond of the area.

But they'd still all be willing to go there if someone needed help.

I'd arrived at the station and we'd received our brief. The crew was picked and I was allocated as shore crew, preparing the boat and checking equipment like the radar, radios, night vision and torches, while the lifeboat crew got into their warmest personal kit: thermals, a thick fleece undersuit (known colloquially by crew as the 'woolly bear') and the yellow RNLI-issue drysuit, along with neoprene gloves and helmet with visor – enough to ward off hypothermia in the North Sea for at least two hours. It was miserable and damp, with the kind of misty rain that meant poor visibility, but at least the sea wasn't as rough as it could be at that time of year.

It was the darkness that was going to be the real problem.

Fortunately, our crew were equipped with two thermal-imaging devices. These weren't standard RNLI kit but had been loaned to the station by a kind benefactor who understood the terrain we worked in and how vital they could be in searches like these. They could detect traces of heat and indicate signs of life when all the naked eye could see was darkness for miles. Even finding the faintest outline of a person at sea or trapped among rocks could mean the difference between life and death.

Having a 'day job' in the military, I specialised in the thermal-imaging kit, so as the boat crew kitted up I made it my job to check it over and make sure it was all working properly, before handing it over to the crew and supporting with the launch. Once they left, we all stayed at the station in case the call came in to launch our second lifeboat, the D-class inflatable *Eileen May Loach-Thomas*, and assist the first crew. If the man was found to be trapped under the cliffs and inaccessible by foot from either end, it would be the best boat to get to him.

The search process was painstaking. Listening in over the VHF radio, we could hear the lifeboat crew providing sitreps, or 'situation reports', as they carefully navigated around the areas of shallow breaking water, searching with the thermal imagers and directing the coastguard team towards a faint glimmer. Getting the distance just right was essential. Too close and they risked the boat and crew running into rocks; too far away and they might miss Mike.

We couldn't see what the boat crew were seeing, but we could imagine it. The bright heat signature of the coastguard team exerting themselves, slowly closing in on the faint static heat trace.

But they didn't want to get their hopes up.

After all, the area had form for seeing searches end in tragedy.

It was only when the coastguard team confirmed definitive signs of life that they allowed themselves to feel optimism.

'Yes, we've found him,' we heard the coastguard say over the radio.

But there was no celebration in the boathouse, not yet. It was almost midnight, so the man had been missing for almost 12 hours. He would be wet through, and the temperature had dropped below freezing.

'What's his condition?' we heard the watchkeeper from the Humber Coastguard Maritime Rescue Coordination Centre ask.

'He's cold, but talking to us and otherwise well,' the coastguard team confirmed.

Yes!

A collective sense of relief settled in the boathouse. It turned out that the man had mistakenly turned right rather than left along the beach. Instead of walking towards where he lived, he'd ended up lost. As darkness and the tide crept in, he'd found himself stuck among the rocks at the base of one of the cliffs.

We'd got the result we wanted, but it was only when we were doing the wash-up that I realised there was a missing piece of the puzzle. We'd been looking for a man and his dog, a Jack Russell called Murphy. But only a man had been mentioned in the radio communications.

What had become of the dog?

I soon had an answer of sorts. When the crew returned, one of the lads turned to me as he was making his way out of the station.

'He wasn't with his dog, you know,' he said.

'Really? That's a shame,' I said.

It was sad, but it was puzzling too. Even if a dog wasn't found with his owner, they usually turned up somewhere. Most of the time they ended up getting home before the rescued party. Sometimes there was a much sadder ending. But they almost always turned up.

He'll turn up tomorrow, I thought as I left the station.

Saturday and Sunday morning passed in a sleepy blur, as was often the case after a long, late shout. But as I went about my usual weekend business, spending time with my wife Jo and our two daughters, the missing dog kept popping into my mind.

Maybe it was because my own dog, Ollie, was bounding around me. Ollie was a two-year-old Tibetan Terrier – a shaggy mountain dog, not your usual salty sea dog. Despite the fact that we lived on the beach, he preferred the mountains and snow to the sand and the sea. In fact, he *hated* the water. He would stare at the sea for hours, but if he got wet he'd be furious.

Ollie wasn't my first dog. Growing up, my parents had a big black Labrador called Monty who loved swimming in the North Sea so much that it was impossible to keep him out of it, summer or winter. Throughout my life I was surrounded by my relatives' dogs and I'd had a whole plethora of other pets too – guinea pigs, cats, rabbits, hamsters, the whole works. We were a family of animal lovers and I just couldn't imagine not knowing what had happened to any of them if they'd gone missing.

Especially the dogs. They were just like big furry members of the family.

If my pager went off when I was walking Ollie or had him out with me in the car, he would have to come along with me, and he really enjoyed it. Maybe it was the buzz of the place or the fact that the shore crew would spoil him with tickles and treats while I was out at sea, but whenever we approached the station he'd be pulling on his lead to get up the steps.

I was sure it was true of lifeboat stations everywhere.

Lifeboat dogs were a huge and important part of the RNLI family. That was certainly the case over at our flanking station, RNLI Hartlepool, where I'd been volunteer crew in my teens and early twenties. Butch was a permeant feature there in the 1990s. He was a scruffy but well-loved Terrier that belonged to the lifeboat mechanic and travelled in his classic motorbike sidecar to and from the station.

One day when I was crew there, the pagers had gone off and I was in the middle of town with my parents' dog, Monty, about a mile away from the station. Ordinarily, I'd have flagged down a motorist and asked for a lift to the station, but I couldn't do that with a big, lumbering Labrador in tow. My only choice was to run to the station. At first Monty loved it – it was all a big game to him. Tongue lolling as he bounded at my heels, his eyes said it all.

This is brilliant!

Because other crew would have been in their cars, I assumed others would get there first and launch, but the pager just kept on going and going. I started to run faster and faster, knowing that seconds could cost lives. As I did, Monty started to run out of puff. I looked down at him.

'Come on, Monty,' I said.

But he wasn't finding it fun anymore. Then, as we crashed through the station doors, came the final indignity. There was no one around to look after him. He looked like he needed a drink, but I didn't have time to mess around, so I pulled him into the changing rooms and turned on the shower.

'Get a drink there, boy,' I said apologetically.

As I threw on my kit, I knew that other crew would eventually turn up and he'd be taken care of. The same would happen in any RNLI station. Sure enough, when I returned there was a host of volunteers and their families fawning over him and slipping him dog treats. He was having a great time and I think the unannounced sprint to the station had been forgiven.

It was a favourite memory and one I cherished. But there were so many more. As they flooded back, my mind was drawn back to Mike's dog Murphy once again. Had he managed to make his way home?

The answer came when I was exchanging messages with other crewmates as night fell on the Sunday night. As we chatted back and forth, conversation turned back to Friday's rescue.

'You do know that dog never turned up?' one said.

My heart sank.

'Oh really? That's pretty bad', I replied.

I was genuinely surprised. I was aware from conversations that a lot of people in the community were on the lookout for the dog and were concerned about him.

I was convinced he'd be OK.

My heart went out to Mike, who would be recovering from his own ordeal but was probably still worried sick about Murphy. We didn't know what the pair might have been through together, or what his companionship meant to him. It wasn't just me who found it odd that the dog hadn't been found and speculated as to what had happened. Other crewmates started sharing theories about where he might be.

Some were optimistic.

Under the cliffs, caught by his lead.

Probably waiting for someone to go and get him.

Stuck at the cut-off.

Others were fearing the worst.

He might have drowned on the first high water on Friday.

I'm not hopeful. He'll be three days without food and probably drinking salt water.

I checked the tides for the following day. There was no point heading out in the pitch dark, but the following morning the tide would be out and it would be an ideal time to scour the area.

I'm going to head out and look for him tomorrow, I messaged.

I didn't want it to look like the RNLI were using vital resources to go out and look for a lost Jack Russell, but I knew if word got out to the public that the dog was still missing, sooner or later someone would take matters into their own hands – and that could easily end in tragedy.

But if I just took Ollie for a walk that way ...

This wasn't strictly a decision made as an RNLI crew member. Some of the considerations we have when rescuing animals were there, but it was largely made out of concern for the dog's owners, as a pet owner and animal lover.

Just one with the experience and training to search for him safely.

As I headed to bed I mentioned my idea to Jo.

'I'm going to walk Ollie down by the cliffs in the morning.'

'What?'

'I'm going to see if I can find that dog.'

For a moment, it looked like she might try to talk me out of it, but she could tell my mind was made up.

'OK, just be careful.'

The next morning my eyes pinged open and I was suddenly overwhelmed by a sense that I knew where the dog was. Premonition is too strong a word, but intuitively, and based on everything I knew about the area, I had an idea of where he must have ended up.

There's a stretch of coastline between Saltburn, about five miles from Redcar, and the point where Mike was found. If the dog had started to make his own way back, he could only have been back towards town and the cut-off.

Two things were certain.

He was either trapped or drowned.

Fortunately, it had snowed over the weekend, so the dog would have had something other than salt water to drink, which would have staved off the risk of dehydration. But as for other injuries, who could say?

I decided to focus on staying optimistic.

I pulled on my bright yellow jacket, got in the car with the kids and Ollie, and dropped the girls off at school before heading to the Ship Inn in Saltburn, the point closest to the cliffs that you could get to by car. I spoke to Lisa, the landlady there, who was the owner of three beautiful and energetic fox-red Labradors herself.

'Is the dog still missing then?' she asked, a concerned expression on her face.

'He is, yes.'

'You leave the car here. I do hope you find him.'

'Me too.'

By 9am I was at the cut-off. I had a 2.5-mile stretch to cover and I wanted to do it as quickly as possible. It was a crisp, cold morning and the sky was a brilliant blue. As beautiful as it was, given the risk of falling rocks and slippery, treacherous terrain it really wasn't a place for a leisurely walk.

Although this wasn't an official RNLI job, I'd agreed to check in with my crewmate Nathan Hobday every ten minutes so they knew where I was if any issues arose. I'd brought my kit, and a pocket full of dog treats and a little portable plastic bowl for Ollie, so he had fresh water while we were out. As we headed south-east from Saltburn, though, I could tell he was a little disconcerted. It wasn't somewhere we'd usually walk, and even though he was nimble on the slippery rocks, he was right on my heel rather than bouncing off and sniffing around everything as normal.

178

Perhaps he was aware of the dangers, or maybe he knew we were doing a job.

Either way, he was as good as gold.

As we moved further round the cliff, the terrain became much trickier. Ollie and I did our best to navigate around the smooth boulders that sat on the flat, slippery, weed-covered shelves of rock, known locally as scars, but it wasn't easy to do that and keep pace.

I knew we'd reached Huntcliff just over halfway through the outward route I'd planned because the rocks were much larger and more jagged. I shuddered just looking at them. They were from recent rockfalls and had been the site of much tragedy. I knew that the mobile signal was poor in the area, so I messaged Nathan.

At Huntcliff. Signal might go so proceeding on the route as planned.

OK. Check in when you get your signal back, he replied.

As we walked beneath the cliffs the air was filled with the sound of the waves crashing, the wind blustering and the seabirds squawking. It was noisy down there, but not noisy enough to miss the distinctive bark of a Jack Russell. I knew they were vocal dogs and quite territorial too, so I was hoping he'd see us and follow his instincts to give a warning bark, or even a growl that Ollie might be able to detect.

But two miles in, we hadn't seen or heard a thing.

By the time we reached the point where Mike had been found, my optimism was waning. He didn't seem to be in any of the places where I'd thought he might be stuck. The only other place I could think of was a few grassy areas midway up the cliffs, known locally as 'the greens', where grass had grown over the top of old landslides. There were hundreds of rabbits up there, so it would be like heaven for a Jack Russell.

Rabbits to chase everywhere, sea views and seagull nests.

Why would he ever want to leave?

We hadn't seen anyone so far on our walk, but at Cattersty Sands I saw a man and woman. The man seemed to be holding something in his hands and concentrating really hard. In the air I could see something zipping around.

He was controlling a drone.

'Good morning,' I said with a wave, once I was within earshot.

'Morning,' he replied, then he nodded up to the drone. 'Been looking for Murphy, but no sign of him on the greens.'

'I'm having a look for him too,' I said.

They had travelled from the other direction, from a fishing village called Skinningrove. I didn't know if they had any connection to Mike or his family, but news of his rescue had spread around town, along with the fact that his dog hadn't been found. They were concerned for the animal's well-being. People always were. I explained I was RNLI crew and advised them on the tides, and they reassured me that they would be well clear of the area before mid-tide.

'Can we swap numbers?' I asked. 'We're both down here, so it would be good to be in touch if there are any problems.'

'Of course,' he said.

I let the crew know there was another person under the cliffs and turned around to retrace our steps. Logically, it was unlikely that we'd find the dog past the point where Mike had been found. If he'd been further along he would have been on the beach at Skinningrove – a beautiful, empty beach well used by dog owners who would surely have seen him over the weekend.

Perhaps we'd just missed him.

Or maybe he'd been swept out to sea …

I didn't even want to think about that.

But my heart sank further with every step back towards Saltburn. Taking a route closer to the cliffs but still keeping a distance from where rocks would land if they fell, we stopped every now and again to search the rockfall areas with binoculars before moving on to the next vantage point. We didn't have that much time to linger and look around, though. I wanted to make sure Ollie and I were well clear of the cliffs before the tide came in.

I didn't want to trouble my crewmates with a call-out to rescue us.

Ollie started getting more impatient too. He had been at my heel all morning but now he was pressing ahead. Like me, he probably sensed that we shouldn't be hanging around here. As I walked briskly, taking care not to slip and hurt myself on the wet rocks, I spotted something ahead of us. It wasn't a dog, but a faded orange plastic life ring.

I picked it up and took it with me.

It was awkward to carry and made keeping my balance harder, but I wanted to move it. Objects like that could cause problems during searches, at first appearing to be the thing we might be looking for but turning out to be a waste of time.

It was a small thing, but it could cost lives.

As we rounded the cliff and Saltburn came back into view about two-thirds of the way back, I'd all but given up hope. Then suddenly Ollie's ears pricked up. I crouched down next to him.

'Good boy! Do you hear something?' I said gently. 'Show me.'

Pausing for a moment, I listened. But all I could hear was the sound of the sea creeping closer to us and the seagulls flapping around. I went to stand up, but Ollie remained rigid, focusing intently on something.

What was it?

Then, from the scree slopes beneath the cliff, I heard it too.

Woof! Woooooof!

My heart started to race as I turned towards the slopes and tried to pinpoint where the sound was coming from. It was quiet but distinctive and seemed to be coming from a particular segment of the slope, so I moved closer.

Woof! Woof! Woooooof!

It wasn't the bark of a happy dog. It sounded angry, not to mention scared.

I grabbed my phone to message Nathan.

Dropping a pin in the map on my phone to share my location, I punched in a quick message.

Found a bark. Going to investigate the scree slopes, I wrote. Nathan's reply came instantly.

No heroics, it read.

I nodded to myself. It was reassuring to know he was there and knew where I was.

I continued moving forward slowly, closing in on the sound, until we reached a large pile of fallen rocks. By now the barking was relentless – and vicious.

Woof! Woooooof! Woof! Woooooof!

Ollie started barking back, but then he stopped dead in his tracks, hanging back cautiously. It was as if he was saying, *'This isn't very nice, I'm staying here.'* If I'm being honest, a part of me felt the same. If this was Murphy, I wasn't likely to be able to get him out alone, but I needed to be sure before I called for assistance.

I put down the life ring and, very carefully, I clambered up the pile of rocks and peered over into the crevice formed by a trio of large rocks that had fallen from the cliff. Peering back at me was the face of a very scared-looking black-and-white Jack Russell.

It had to be Murphy.

'Murphy?' I said, to see if he responded to his name.

He did, but not in the way I'd hoped. He burst into a frenzied fit of barking, snapping his jaws and lunging towards me.

'Easy boy,' I said, quickly stepping well back.

But it was clear he was stuck fast, his back end appearing to be trapped by one of the large rocks. I moved around the pile and saw that there was no way that the offending rock could be moved by a single person. I was going to need help.

I grabbed my phone, took a quick snap, then took Ollie's portable water bowl from my bag and quickly dropped it in front of the trapped dog, along with a few dog biscuits. I didn't want to get too close but was conscious he might be hungry and thirsty. As it landed in front of him, the dog started barking wildly again.

Ollie joined in too.

Once the dog had calmed down a little I retreated down the scree slope to a safer position, then grabbed my phone and sent the photo of Murphy to Nathan. It was 10.41am, and coming up to two hours after I'd started my search.

No way. What do you need? he messaged back.

The dog was yapping away again, baring his sharp teeth and lunging forward.

Welders gloves, I replied, only half joking.

I can be there in 15 minutes, he said.

Knowing help was on the way, my mind instantly went to Mike. He still had no idea what had become of Murphy. I was concerned that the poor dog's legs might have been crushed by the rock, but even if that were the case, the dog was alive. We just might need to get him some help if he was hurt. Had it been me, I knew I'd want to know the moment Ollie had been found, regardless of the state he was in, so I typed another message.

Let the family know. And get an appointment at Saltburn vets.

At 10.43am Nathan messaged again.

Will do. Do you need me to come through with the gloves?

At the time I was messaging the drone operator to let him know the dog had been found. With the tide coming in, I wanted to be sure they were well clear of any danger too. By the time I went to reply to Nathan, he'd sent another message.

On way with Cameron, he said at 10.45am.

Ten minutes later he messaged again.

ETA 10 mins. Jordan S also coming.

Cameron Bond was another experienced RNLI volunteer, who was strong from hauling lobster pots on his fishing boat and knew every inch of the cliffs as well as I did. Jordan Summersgill was an off-duty coastguard volunteer, owner of both a dog and a local pet shop called Nibblers, so I knew her experience would come in useful too.

As I waited for help to arrive, I looked around me. The ominous cliffs with their precariously balanced loads started to look increasingly familiar. Then suddenly I realised. It was almost exactly the same spot where I'd almost been hit by a falling rock when I was out on a shout a couple of years earlier. A knot tightened in my stomach as I was reminded of just how dangerous this stretch of coast was.

We needed to stay safe, but I didn't want to lose the dog's position. If he stopped barking we would probably never find him again safely among the vast numbers of rocks. The huge scree slopes were notorious for being a difficult place to locate casualties. It was the reason I'd chosen to wear my bright yellow coat.

Just in case.

Suddenly I had a thought. What happened if I couldn't find him again? There were thousands of piles of rocks and they all looked the same. I needed to find a way to mark the spot.

Then I saw it. The orange life ring, lying on the ground beside me.

I'm glad I picked this up, I thought as I grabbed it and scrambled the 20 metres back up to the spot where Murphy was stuck.

Once it was in a clear, visible position, I clambered back down.

'Come on, Ollie,' I said, guiding him back towards the sea, well away from the scree slopes and the risk of falling rocks. From a distance of about 50 metres, the ring was like a dot among the scree and swathes of light-grey rocks, which were clearly from a recent rockfall. Suddenly it dawned on me. There must have been a rockfall on the night Mike went missing.

Murphy must have been caught up in it.

Soon after, Nathan, Cameron and Jordan arrived with some thick gloves. They'd driven from the Ship Inn as far as the cut-off in a 4×4 pick-up truck to save time.

We huddled together to make a plan.

'We don't know how injured the dog is,' I said. 'I think his legs might be crushed.'

'But if they're not he might make a run for it when we move the rock,' Nathan said.

'Exactly,' I replied.

We decided to roll the rock off the dog as quickly as we could, then slip Ollie's lead on him if he tried to bolt away. There really wasn't much else we could do. Nathan and Cameron took the rock, while Jordan and I got ready to catch him.

'One, two, three,' I counted quietly, trying my best not to spook the dog.

With a great collective heave, we managed to roll the rock away. There was a flurry of activity and somehow Jordan managed to loop Ollie's red slip lead over the dog's head.

'Got him!' she said.

'Nice work,' I replied.

Miraculously, Murphy seemed to be uninjured.

He was like a different dog too, immediately calm. It looked like he'd just been trapped by one foot and unable to wriggle out from under the rocks. At some point while he was struggling, his collar must have come off, as we found it lying under the rocks.

He didn't touch the water I'd put out for him, so I could only assume he'd quenched his thirst by licking the snow that

186

had fallen around him. The biscuits went untouched too, but I don't think I'd have much of an appetite after the ordeal of being stuck alone under a rock for three days either.

Once he was freed, I grabbed the big plastic bag I'd put in my pack. I'd anticipated every eventuality when I'd gathered my kit together and the bag had been added just in case I found myself having to bring the dog's body back with me. Instead, I put him in it to keep him warm, like marathon runners do with tinfoil blankets at the end of a race. I wrapped one of our RNLI blankets around him too, for comfort and as an extra layer to help him warm back up.

He didn't even flinch; he just looked up at me with those big black eyes. I carried him carefully in my arms down the scree slope with the others helping to support me and Ollie trotting over the rocks with ease. Once we reached the flat of the scars, we made sure we hadn't left anything and then started walking back towards safety on the firm sand on the other side of the cut-off, where Cameron had parked his pick-up truck. I was absolutely filthy, so I sat in the load bed cradling Murphy, with Nathan next to me and Ollie sitting between us.

As Cameron slowly drove us back to the Ship Inn, with our arms also around Ollie, we patted Murphy gently. He relaxed completely, but Ollie still had his reservations about Murphy. I think he knew he wasn't a bad dog, just a very scared one that might not welcome having him around.

'Good boy, Ollie,' I said as he sat patiently in the truck. Then I turned back to Murphy.

'You're all right Murphy,' I said, petting him gently. 'Let's get you home.'

Word travelled fast in town, and by the time we arrived back in Saltburn news of the rescue was all over social media and a crowd had gathered, including Murphy's two owners. As I passed Murphy to Nathan and bundled out of the truck, I could see both of their faces light up. And when Nathan handed him over?

The expressions on their faces conveyed an emotion I could completely understand.

The deepest sense of relief you could imagine.

That dog was a member of their family, and he'd been missing for two days and three nights. They must have been at their wits' end. I popped Ollie on his lead and crouched down next to him to feed him a biscuit. Ruffling his big fluffy head, I nuzzled into him.

'Good dog. Well done today,' I said.

I was so proud of him, as he'd behaved perfectly. And he'd helped us to find Murphy.

I wished I could have stayed longer and chatted more with the family, but the whole escapade had taken longer than I'd expected. I was working from home, and by the time I'd got back and changed I was a couple of hours late logging on to my online meetings.

As I got my head down into my work, Ollie lay his head down on the kitchen floor.

He was absolutely exhausted.

'Sorry,' I said to my team, 'I was out rescuing a dog.'

If they didn't know that I was RNLI crew, they probably wouldn't have believed me. The story got quite a lot of attention anyway, so all the evidence was out there on social media and in the press. In the days that followed donations poured in for the station.

It's incredible how people respond to animal rescues. When it comes to humans, people seem to find it easier, rightly or wrongly, to make judgements and assign blame for others getting into trouble. Animals are innocent and vulnerable, and when we rescue one, we tend to get behind it together, while human rescues sometimes divide people.

A few days later we heard that Murphy had a clean bill of health from the vet and was doing brilliantly. It was a fantastic feeling because, looking back, between the rockfall and the tides, the fact that he was found safe and well really was against all the odds. Events like this really do make you appreciate your own pets more. Whenever I creep back into the house after a late shout, leaving the lights off and trying not to disturb anyone, Ollie still pads from his dog bed near the back door to quietly come and stretch his paws up onto me as if to say, *Glad you're home*, before heading straight back to bed. It's a little acknowledgement that feels all the more special now.

12

ALL AT SEA

Myles Hussey, Cowes,
July 2021

It was a calm, clear Saturday morning on the Solent, the strait in the English Channel between the mainland coast of Hampshire and the north coast of the Isle of Wight. I'd brought two of our trainee crew, Jean-Marc Bonello and Flic Elliott, out on an extra training exercise to give them a little more practice in the basics of boat handling and navigation as they progressed towards their RNLI assessments.

We'd already practised anchoring and a bit of towing, and now I wanted to put their navigation skills to the test.

'I'd like you to put a safe passage from Cowes over to Stanswood Bay into the e-nav,' I said. 'But when we're out there, we'll try some blind navigation.'

Blind navigation was finding your way using just the radar, something you'd need to do if you were out on a shout and the e-nav system was knocked off or you couldn't use it because it was foggy.

It didn't seem all that long since I'd been doing the same exercises myself.

I'd joined Cowes RNLI about four years earlier. I'd gone out fishing many times in the Solent with my grandad and we'd often see the lifeboat going out. I'd been desperate to join the lifeboat crew. When my opportunity came I took it, and after two years as shore crew I progressed to boat crew on our Atlantic 85 inshore lifeboat, the *Sheena Louise*.

I was so excited when I was made helm, but it's a huge responsibility too. At first I was hesitant, but I decided it was better to have a go and see if I was up to it rather than not trying at all. I love it and I really enjoy helping novice crew progress in the same way that I was helped myself.

In the few years I'd been with the RNLI, I'd seen a lot of different types of shouts. Cowes and the Solent have a huge yachting community, so I'd ticked off plenty of towing jobs, jammed sails, broken-down ships and vessels that had run aground on Brambles Bank and other notorious sandbanks in the area. I'd also done my fair share of rescuing people and medical evacuations, but there was one tasking I *still* hadn't done. An animal rescue.

I had dogs of my own, two Blue Whippets called Tilly and Winnie, and I adored them. I'd watched so many pet rescues on *Saving Lives at Sea* and seen how overwhelmed owners were when they were reunited with their pets, and I knew how much someone helping my dogs would mean to me. While I hadn't been out on one yet, dog rescues weren't uncommon and I knew I'd be called to lend a hand at some point.

Flic and Jean-Marc were coping well with my initial instructions. They'd both been out on a couple of shouts, so had lots of observational experience and were learning fast. I decided to challenge them a bit.

'Right, we now need a safe passage back to Newtown Creek. Can you put it in?' I said. 'Make sure we stay out of the precautionary area.'

The precautionary area ran from North East Gurnard across to Gurnard North and then Prince Consort. It was the area in which big shipping operated, the massive ships needing ample space to turn, so we had to keep ourselves and others clear at all times. As Flic and Jean-Marc got to work, I watched and offered suggestions, but they were doing really well. Once that exercise was complete, we decided to work on a bit of close-quarter boat handling.

'Let's head back to the River Medina,' I said, taking the helm.

With the waters still calm, I put the throttle on full and powered in the direction of the river. We were going about 30 knots and making good progress when I suddenly glimpsed something out the corner of my eye, about two or three car lengths from the boat. Jean-Marc saw it too.

'What's that?' he said.

I brought the boat to a complete stop and turned my head to get a proper look. There was something that seemed to be floating, beam on to our starboard side. It was brown and low in the water, but I couldn't quite make it out.

Was it a log?

Suddenly, the 'log' appeared to move.

'Is it an animal?' Flic said. 'I think it's an animal.'

195

Well, it certainly wasn't a log. Or a person.

'Is it a dog?' I wondered out loud.

It was entirely possible that a dog had entered the water from the shore, got caught by the tide and been swept out, but from a distance it didn't look like any breed I recognised. Slowly, I brought the boat round to get a better look. I squinted as we approached the unidentified object. It was a little bit bigger than a Great Dane, but it had a rough, red-brown coat, a pointed muzzle – and a pair of bumps on the top of its head ...

It wasn't a dog at all!

'That's a deer!' I said to Jean-Marc and Flic, as I gawped in disbelief.

'No way,' Jean-Marc said.

'It one-hundred-per-cent is,' I said, inching a bit closer. 'It's a blooming deer.'

'Oh my goodness, so it is!' said Flic.

'What *are* you doing out here, mate?' I said, staring at the soggy creature, which seemed ... well, all at sea. Its legs were going ten to the dozen as it swam around helplessly, one and a half miles from land. All of a sudden our training exercise had switched gear into a real-life animal rescue.

I quickly assessed the situation. The deer was in the precautionary area. There was a yacht tacking towards us and I could see the Red Funnel ferry on its usual route between East Cowes and Southampton. I started waving the yacht off its intended course and grabbed the radio to call the coastguard.

'Solent Coastguard, this is Cowes Lifeboat,' I said. 'Just to inform you, we have located a deer swimming in the precautionary area in the Solent.'

There was silence for a moment, then the radio crackled into life.

'Can you please confirm what you've just said?' she said.

'Yes, no problem,' I replied. 'We have located a *deer* in the precautionary area.' I put as much emphasis on the word 'deer' as possible.

'A deer?' the coastguard replied, sounding thoroughly bemused.

'Yes, a deer,' I confirmed.

After repeating myself three times, they finally believed what they were hearing. But they still seemed confused. To be honest, I was too. I had no idea how the animal had managed to get out here, presumably swept three miles across the Solent from the New Forest.

'OK, what are your intentions?' the coastguard asked.

We hadn't been tasked to rescue the animal and at present there was no risk to human life, so it was up to us to decide the best and safest course of action.

Well, I'm not going to let the poor thing swim around until it drowns or gets hit by something, am I? It's up to us to save it, I thought.

'We're going to try to herd it back towards Cowes,' I said.

'OK, go ahead,' the Coastguard said.

I started to manoeuvre the boat, with Jean-Marc and Flic positioned to 'shoo' the deer in the right direction. But after a couple of minutes it was clear that this wasn't working. The poor thing was spinning around, legs flailing, and fighting to keep his head above water.

'Nah, he's struggling,' I said. 'It's not fair on him doing it this way.'

'What should we do?' asked Flic.

'Let's get him on board,' I said.

I confirmed our new intention to the coastguard, then turned my attention to exactly *how* we were going to get the creature onto the boat. He wasn't like a dog or domestic animal, who was used to having people around and would be wearing a collar or lead we could grab. We had no idea how he would react to being handled, and the last thing we wanted was a scared and angry deer kicking about in the lifeboat.

But the deer was actually swimming *towards* the boat. He was more scared of being in the water than he was of us, and you could see the energy draining out of him. Every paddle of his hooves seemed laboured and his head was dipping below the water with alarming regularity. He was being swamped by the water.

'Right, gloves on and visors down,' I said. 'Let's get him on board.'

Flic and Jean-Marc didn't need telling twice.

I positioned the lifeboat so we were beam on to the deer. As we came alongside him, his head was stretching pleadingly towards the sky and he was panting heavily. Flic and Jean-Marc leaned over and grabbed him, but because the deer was so low in the water he slipped out of their grasp.

'He's going towards the stern,' Flic said, as the animal paddled away.

The back of the boat was lower, about four inches from the waterboard, so he must have realised that was an easier route to get on deck.

Smart deer!

But the engines were there too, and our propellers. In training, it was vital to communicate to the helm the moment anyone looked like they were going near the engines, to avoid serious injuries. I knocked the boat into neutral and turned the wheel, so the boat pivoted to meet the deer as he came round. With a route to safety in his sights, you could see the steely determination on the little deer's face as he started swimming straight towards the engines.

'He's coming up to the engines,' Jean-Marc said.

'He's between the engines,' Flic added a few seconds later.

Flic and Jean-Marc's training was shining through.

It was all perfect procedure. Especially for two novices who'd found themselves thrown into a rescue!

'No problem,' I said, holding the boat in position.

'I'm going to grab him,' Flic said.

As she did I heard a sudden slopping noise, followed by an almighty burst of squawking and spluttering. I turned my head.

The deer was on board.

Now we just had to keep him calm and still.

'Flic,' I said, 'let's get him to the bow and settle him there, away from the engines.'

We'd need our power back to get him to shore as quickly as possible, and we didn't want to risk any injuries if he fell or jumped back in.

It's a good thing that Flic was a doctor in her day job. She wasn't scared or squeamish about anything, she just rolled her sleeves up and got stuck in. As she moved the deer along the boat with Jean-Marc's help, I kept a close eye on proceedings.

'Keep him low,' I said. 'If he starts kicking, he's either going to hit one of us or go back over.'

'OK,' she said, shuffling him along to the front of the boat.

A minute or two later, she'd done it.

'What now?' she asked.

I looked at her sitting at the bow with the deer more or less lying in her lap. It was the most unusual situation I'd ever experienced with the RNLI. What *were* we meant to do next? There were no drills or procedures for deer rescue. I thought hard.

What would we do with a human casualty?

'Let's get the ambulance pouch,' I said. 'Put it over him, make sure it's dark and keep him warm.'

'OK, got it,' she said, as Jean-Marc passed her the pouch.

Once the deer was safely in he seemed to calm down. But we couldn't be complacent. I considered tying his legs up, just to be on the safe side, but we were less than ten minutes from shore and it seemed unnecessary. Looking at its head poking out of the pouch, with Flic holding him and whispering gently into his ear, I realised that the poor thing was absolutely shattered.

He wasn't going anywhere any time soon.

'Just hold onto him,' I said, 'so he doesn't kick off.'

I grabbed the radio and called the coastguard to update him on our status.

'We've recovered the deer to the boat,' I said.

'OK, so what are your intentions now?' she asked.

Errrr … I thought.

It was a good question. What *did* you do with a rescued wild deer? Once again, we were in completely new territory.

'We're closest to Cowes,' I said. 'Can you inform our deputy launching authority [DLA] that we have a deer on board?'

After all, we'd gone out on a training exercise, not a rescue. I didn't want to turn up at the station unannounced with a distressed deer.

'Yes, we'll inform them,' she said.

'Can you get the RSPCA to the station too, please?' I asked.

'Of course,' she said.

I knew we were going to need a little help deciding what to do next …

Usually after an exercise we'd do a fuel run and pick up any empty jerry cans from the pontoon, fill them up and recover the boat, ready for her next service. But there was no way I was going to try to take the deer off on the pontoon. There was every chance he would run off into Cowes – or back to the water and get into trouble again.

We needed to keep him safe until the RSPCA arrived.

I radioed the station. I'd tried to keep it all low-key, knowing that a deer turning up at the station would generate a lot of curiosity, but word of the incoming animal had still spread.

'We're coming straight into the boathouse,' I said. 'We'll unload the deer there.'

'OK,' came the response.

As we powered back towards the shore, I looked at the creature strewn across the bow. He looked so small and vulnerable, but calm as well. It was impossible not to feel for the little guy. Truth be told, I was getting quite attached to him.

'He needs a name,' I said. 'We can't just call him "the deer", can we?'

'Does he look like an Elvis, maybe?' Flic said.

'What about Reg?' suggested Jean-Marc.

Then suddenly I had it. We'd found him on the ebbing tide.

'Let's call him Ebbing,' I said.

In the end we decided on Ebbing Cowes, to recognise the tide he was swimming in and the location he was rescued to. It was perfect – and it suited him too!

As we came in, the Red Funnel ferry was on its way out, giving its passengers a bird's-eye view of the inside of our boat. You could see the surprise on their faces as they stared at the big orange ambulance pouch with a little animal head sticking out.

As they puzzled over what the creature might be, I was planning our next steps.

'We'll take Ebbing off and get him straight into the shower block,' I said to Flic and Jean-Marc. 'We can keep it nice and dark, and have a water bowl and a warm blanket for him in there.'

Once we were in the boathouse, I climbed off the lifeboat and Flic passed the deer down to me, still in the pouch. Exactly as we expected, there were plenty of crew at the station keen to see the deer that had mysteriously appeared in the Solent.

'Time for your photo opportunity, Ebbing,' I said gently.

Making sure my visor was securely down, I shuffled him out of the pouch, put one hand under his body and round his legs to keep him still, then placed his head in the crook of my other arm, hand protectively placed on his body.

'Just give him a bit of space,' I said, as a few photos were taken.

When we popped Ebbing in the shower room he just took a drink from the water bowl we'd put out and lay down on the cool floor.

'Let's leave him to rest,' I said.

We still didn't know how long the RSPCA were going to be, so we put a sign up on the bathroom to warn crew members of our special visitor.

Do not enter. Deer resting.

Truth be told, I knew it would more likely encourage them to peek in, but I just didn't want anyone scaring or disturbing Ebbing. As I headed to the mess room, Anne, our DLA, spotted me.

'You've still got to do the fuel run,' she reminded me.

'Oh yeah,' I said. 'I'll get that done now.'

In all the excitement, I'd almost forgotten.

'Do me a favour, though, Anne,' I said. 'If the RSPCA come, please don't let them take Ebbing until I'm back. I want to say my goodbyes.'

'Of course,' Anne said with a smile.

It sounds daft, but I really felt like I'd bonded with Ebbing and I didn't want him to just disappear. I think I managed my fastest boat recovery ever that day, spurred on by the thought of missing Ebbing leaving. As I finished up, I bumped into Mark Southwell, our lifeboat operations manager (LOM). He knew just about every rescue that the station had seen, so I asked him a question.

'Please tell me this is our first deer rescue,' I said.

'Yep,' he said. 'I can confirm the island has never had a deer rescue. This is a first.'

'Yes!' I said.

Ebbing was going to be famous!

I dashed back into the station and bumped into the DLA again.

'Is he still there?' I said, a knot tightening in my stomach.

'Yes, he's still there,' she said.

'Oh good,' I said, the knot releasing.

I hadn't missed him.

As we waited for the RSPCA, I checked in on him every few minutes. He was so good. When I opened the door, he just cocked his head and looked over at me – no trying to run out, no kicking about. As time passed and he slowly recovered, he became more and more perky, standing upright and tapping around the shower cubicle.

Eventually, a man from the RSPCA arrived. I put my cup of tea down and walked over to him.

'You've come about the deer?' I asked.

'Yes,' he said.

'He's in here,' I said, indicating for him to follow me to the shower room.

He opened the door, peered in and nodded knowingly.

'Yes, that looks like a Muntjac deer,' he said. 'They're usually found in the New Forest, though, not in the Solent!'

'It was a surprise for us too,' I said.

'I'm just going to have to get my big crate for him,' he said.

'I'll give you a hand,' I offered.

We brought the crate in from his van, then the next moment he started putting layers of clothes on, all topped off with a big jacket.

'You cold, mate?' I asked.

'No, no,' he said seriously, as he grabbed a thick blanket. 'These deer do get aggressive. They can rip you to pieces with their hooves and antlers.'

I just couldn't imagine it. I didn't like to mention that Ebbing didn't have antlers yet either, just those two little spuds sticking out of his head. He was the professional, though, so I let him crack on. I opened the shower-room door for him, and watched as he walked in and threw the blanket over the deer. It must have been usual procedure for them, but Ebbing didn't like it one bit.

He went absolutely mad.

The man quickly left the shower room and shut the door as Ebbing ran round and round in circles. By now Flic was watching as well.

'He wasn't aggressive in the boat,' she said, her concern clear in her voice.

'To be fair, he had just swum three miles across the Solent then,' I said.

'True,' she agreed. 'Got a bit of fight to him now.'

I knew the RSPCA guy was right to take precautions, but I couldn't help thinking there might be a better way. After a few attempts using his method, I decided to step in.

'Mate, any chance I can have a go?' I said.

'Yeah, all right,' he said.

I opened the door and walked into the shower room.

Ebbing seemed to tense up initially, but then I think he recognised me. No blanket, no extra padding, just myself in my regular RNLI gear. I stayed back but brought the cage a little closer. Crouching down, I looked him in the eye.

'In you go, Ebbing,' I said, tapping the cage just above its door and gesturing with my head. Ebbing looked up at me, then looked at the cage, sizing up the situation.

In the end, he decided to trust me.

Obediently, he clip-clopped across the tiles and walked straight into the cage.

'Good boy, Ebbing,' I said, closing the door behind him.

Picking up the cage, I passed it to the RSPCA officer.

'Here you go, mate,' I said.

'Good work,' he smiled. 'Thanks.'

I knew I'd bonded with Ebbing, and here was the proof. As they packed him off into the van, and Flic and I said our goodbyes, I started to feel a bit sad.

'Here's the contact number for our LOM,' I said to the man. 'Let us know how he gets on.'

'I'll try and keep you posted,' he said.

'Bye, Ebbing Cowes,' I said as they drove away.

As I walked back to the station, I was stopped by a group of people who'd seen the cage being moved.

'What did you have there?' one asked. 'Did I see a little paw?'

'A hoof,' I smiled. 'It was a deer.'

'A deer?!' someone else exclaimed.

'Yes, a deer,' I repeated, for about the hundredth time that day. 'Here, have a look.'

I took my phone out and proudly showed off the picture of

Ebbing being lifted from the boat. I was as bad as I was with my dogs. A proud pet parent.

When I finally arrived home later that day, I told my partner Kylea all about my day and my rather exotic animal rescue.

I knew we might not find out exactly how Ebbing got on and that he might need some time in a shelter to recuperate from his ordeal, but I knew he was in good hands with the RSPCA. I was also confident that I, Flic, Jean–Marc and the rest of the Cowes RNLI crew had done our very best for him. I was sure he'd be running free back where he belonged in no time.

I knew word had spread about Ebbing, but the response was ridiculous the following day. My photo with Ebbing was splashed all over the local media and even the national press. My phone didn't stop beeping with messages.

'Hey, mate. You're famous.'

My reply each time was the same.

'I'm not famous. Ebbing is!'

Ebbing Cowes, the first deer ever to be rescued by our lifeboat station – I was just the bloke in the picture holding him.

As my maiden animal rescue, it was such an extraordinary experience. Our trainee crew responded brilliantly to everything the situation threw at them and I really couldn't have been prouder of what we achieved that day.

13

CAUGHT IN THE BAY

*Chris Winzar and Jamie Mathys,
Salcombe and Dart,
March and April 2017*

The whale was an unexpected visitor to the area. Even after being with the RNLI for 26 years, both at Salcombe and as a full-time staff coxswain covering stations around the country, and working as crew on big yachts all over the world, I'd never seen anything quite like it.

Normally humpback whales are found in the seas off Scandinavia or New England, not the UK's south-west coast. But for some reason this one had chosen to hang around the waters of Start Bay in Slapton, south Devon. The story made the local and even national press, and people travelled from all over to try to catch a glimpse. We were aware of the creature's movements, but I don't think any of us expected the call that came in. I was already in the station when my pager sprang to life.

Launch ALB [all-weather lifeboat].

As the crew arrived at the station and kitted up, more information came in from the coastguard. We were being tasked to assist crew from our flanking station, RNLI Dart, who were attending an ongoing incident.

The whale was stuck.

'It's caught in a line of whelk pots in Start Bay,' the coast-guard explained.

It had been trying to feed with its calf in the shallows and found itself trapped in the fishing lines that were attached to the pots. Dart's inshore lifeboat (ILB) had been called to carry British Divers Marine Life Rescue (BDMLR) to the whale, after a fishing boat belonging to the owner of the pots had raised the alarm. Between them they were working to cut the whale free. It was a dangerous job and we were required to stand by, ready to help.

As we headed out on our Tamar-class all-weather lifeboat, the *Baltic Exchange III*, we weren't entirely sure what that help might look like, or if it would be needed at all. One thing we did know was that when dealing with a wild animal of that size, everything could change in a split second.

We arrived at the scene about 30 minutes later.

'Stand back, Chris,' the coastguard advised us when we were a few hundred metres away from Dart's inshore lifeboat.

It was positioned with its engine over a patch of dark water. As we stopped and held our own position, we saw the divers in black wetsuits leaning over the sides. Larger waves started to roll under the boat, then the whale appeared. Head struggling to break the surface of the waves, it forced air out through its blowhole, its body dwarfing the five-and-a-half-metre-long lifeboat.

They were sitting directly on top of it.

As they tried to get the marine divers as close as possible to cut the lines, the risk became apparent. One flick of the mammal's tail could easily capsize the ILB. As much as we were there to help free the animal, we were there to protect the crew from RNLI Dart, the divers and the crew on the fishing boat too.

The poor animal had been stuck for several hours now and despite a few attempts to free it, the first hadn't been successful. The lines were still wrapped around its tail, and, as it thrashed around, the pots were sinking straight to the sea bed, weighing it down. If we didn't work fast the poor thing was bound to drown.

'We need to try a different approach,' Dart said over the radio.

Within minutes a new plan was proposed. Instead of sitting over the whale, it was decided that the line from the pots would be used to pull the whale towards the fishing boat. One of the divers would then hang from the side of the fishing vessel while a winch lifted the whale's tail as high as possible out of the water, enabling the diver to cut the line that way. It was certainly no less risky, but it was more practical.

'We'll bring crew over to assist,' I said.

We pulled alongside the fishing boat and two of my crew climbed on board, joining the divers and crew from Dart, who had also boarded. Once again I stood the ALB back and waited, ready to swing into action should any of the crew or divers find themselves in trouble. After all, with the lines from the pots attached to a 15-tonne animal, it would only take the diver's foot getting caught up in one of them and the whale deciding to go back down for the man to be submerged along with it.

While they took care of the animal, we were there primarily to protect human life.

The whale had initially been coming to the surface every three to five minutes, but the more it struggled and became entangled in the lines, the more agitated it became. By the time the marine diver started to climb down the side of the boat, the whale was coming to the surface every two minutes or so.

The tension was immense. One misstep and the diver could end up in the water. While the marine divers had training in whale rescue, this was the first time they'd had to put it into practice. For the RNLI, this was a first too. The crew on the boat set into position, pulling on the line that would lift the whale's tail.

My heart was in my mouth as the diver grasped a rail in his right hand and rooted his feet on top of the grey fishing boat's fender. Once steady, he leaned down until he was almost at a 90-degree angle, his side directly above the animal.

Then, clutching a small, sharp knife in his left hand, he looked around, trying to work out the position of the whale and locate the line that needed cutting. But the motion of the boat as the whale writhed about made it a tricky task for both the diver and the crew pulling with all their might on deck.

As the diver reached out towards the rope, the whale, still trying to free itself, jerked away, bouncing the boat. I inhaled sharply as the diver lost his footing. His body swung back towards the boat and his feet slipped below the fender. There was a flurry of movement as the diver's left hand and feet slipped and slid as they tried to reconnect with the boat. His bottom even almost touched the animal's body, but at the last moment he managed to get his feet back onto the fender. I exhaled as he steadied himself again.

214

Thank goodness, I thought.

As the whale attempted to come up again, still tethered by the lines and pots, the diver took his next opportunity. Cutting towards the boat, so as not to injure the whale, he swiped at the rope, his hand disappearing into the water.

When the line reappeared above the waves, it was starting to fray.

Almost there.

A moment later he sliced again, then again, until the rope was completely cut.

In one great movement, the whale – realising it was free – pulled away.

Relief washed over me, not just for the whale, but for the crew and divers too. As it sped off, it breached, bellowing a jet of spray into the air. It was an incredible sight and a brilliant feeling. If we, Dart and the divers hadn't gone to its aid, I doubted that it would have survived much longer.

But as it sped away, I noticed that it still had all kinds of gear attached to its tail and fins.

Would this stuff cause problems, or would it shake it all off?

In the days that followed there was all sorts of talk at the station and around town about the whale rescue. It seemed like a once-in-a-lifetime kind of shout. But knowing all those lines were still attached to the whale niggled at me. If it found itself swimming in among more lines it could easily get stuck again. What would happen then?

I wanted to believe everything was fine, but I could feel it in my gut:

We hadn't seen the last of that whale.

I was walking down the steps to the boathouse when my pager went off. We were actually meeting at the lifeboat station in Dart to set up a barbecue for one of the crew's birthday celebrations.

But when the pager sounded …

Our D-class lifeboat, *Spirit of the Dart*, was already out after being tasked to a shout on the river, but a few of the other crew were at the station, setting up for the social later that evening. We all gathered round to find out what was going on.

'You won't believe it,' Chris said.

'What? Go on,' I said.

'The whale's back. It's stuck again,' he said.

'No way,' I replied. I really couldn't believe it.

About a week earlier, the humpback whale rescue was all anyone was talking about. It was right that you didn't get to go out on every job, we all understood that. But some shouts were special and if you weren't around or on the boat, you always wished you'd been there. That was how I'd felt about the whale shout.

Seeing a creature like that so close up and helping to rescue it would be special.

Maybe even a once-in-a-lifetime job.

But apparently John Fenton, our volunteer press officer, had received a call from the owner of Blackpool Sands, a private beach west of Dartmouth, reporting that the whale was stuck again. John had tried to call various crew members.

But it was 1 April.

Everyone had thought he was winding us up and pulling an April Fool's joke. They'd laughed him off – until he called the coastguard and the shout came in, that is.

Launch ILB.

The D-class was on its way back in, after a long shout. So rather than heading straight out again to the whale, the lifeboat operations manager instructed us to do a crew change. I was a helm and I was already at the station, so I took the boat. Chris Tracey – also a helm, and who had been on the previous whale shout – was at the station, and volunteers Will Davies and Mark Conroy were both nearby, so they joined me.

We kitted up, and after a speedy changeover with the incoming crew we were ready to launch.

It looked like I was going to get close up to this whale after all.

As we left the pontoon, a few minutes after the call came in, the reality of going out to assist a 15-tonne wild animal began to sink in. I was an Essex boy who'd moved to Dartmouth with my wife 12 years earlier to learn to sail. We loved the community here, and me joining the RNLI crew was a huge part of that, so we never left. In the summer of 2005 we'd sailed around Britain and the west coast of Ireland and seen all kinds of marine life, but never a humpback whale. In fact, the only place I'd ever seen one was probably in the Natural History Museum in London.

My mind lurched from *This is exciting, I'm going to see a whale* to *What's this actually going to be like?* in a matter of seconds, although I knew it was really special.

But it was also potentially really dangerous.

I'd been crew with the RNLI for eleven years and a helm for seven. As a helm, you are ultimately responsible for the

217

boat and your crew. Your main job is to make sure you get out, do what we need to do and get the crew back safely.

With every shout, once you were on your way you had a few minutes to develop a picture in your mind as to what you were going to find, how you were going to react and what exactly you were going to do. This one was no different. I focused and got my head in gear.

What were the risks?

What could go wrong?

How could I keep my crew safe?

Given that both Dart and Salcombe had been out to the whale once, we already had a certain amount of knowledge. The crews had talked about the size and power of the animal – if it flicked its tail it could seriously damage the boat or send someone overboard and it wouldn't even notice us, let alone feel us.

It would be like nothing more than scratching an itch.

At least that knowledge was something. We knew that we couldn't be complacent. Not for one second.

It took about ten minutes to reach the position just off Blackpool Sands. The first thing I saw was Salcombe's all-weather lifeboat, then I saw the whale. Or part of it, at least. Its 'hump' was protruding above the waterline, waves lapping around it. I couldn't see its tail and it didn't seem to be moving around too much, but I could see its outline. It was big.

It was very, very big.

Although it was a daunting sight, the crew were calm. We knew we just had to approach the job like any other. Same techniques, different context.

And a very different animal.

Once we were a few hundred metres away from the whale and the all-weather lifeboat, I radioed the Salcombe crew to see how they wanted us to play it. They were leading the operation and we were there to support their plan. From a distance I could see they were using the boat's heavy-duty winch to hoist the lines of pots up, but they couldn't really get down to the waterline to cut them off. They were too high up. The D-class sat low in the water, so we could help there. We radioed the ALB.

'Dart Lifeboat to Salcombe, standing by and ready to assist,' I said.

'If we hoist the pots, you can come alongside and cut the lines,' Salcombe's coxswain Chris Winzar said. He'd been on the first shout and worked alongside Chris Tracey from our crew, so both already had some experience of dealing with the whale.

'No problem,' we responded.

We didn't want to just let go of the pots and leave them dropping to the bottom, so we decided that once the lines were cut the Salcombe crew would pull the pots aboard their boat and take them back to shore.

We needed people in a variety of different positions to make the plan work, so we transferred one of our crew to Salcombe's boat to help with hoisting the pots. Next we headed to the beach to collect one of the BDMLR team. She would assist the ILB crew in cutting the lines as quickly as possible.

'I'll get in the water to make it easier to get to the lines,' she said, once we were back out. I looked at the whale and then at the all-weather lifeboat. As I did, the whale rose to the surface, higher than it had since we'd arrived. It was the first time I'd really seen the mess it was in. Momentarily I was overwhelmed by a sense of sadness.

Lines were twisted and tangled around its tail and fins, whelk pots hanging off it and pulling it down from every angle. This magnificent creature, a giant of the sea, was reduced to flailing around in a 25-metre area, tethered by fishing gear.

It was heartbreaking.

A truly sad, sorry sight. And its situation was worsening. Suddenly, it let out a high-pitched whine and air came shooting out of its blowhole.

The whale was fighting for breath.

We needed to be quick, but I had to consider safety too. The creature was more or less right up to the boat. If a person were in the water it would only take the slightest flick or twist and they'd be crushed between the boat and the whale. I turned to the diver and shook my head.

'We do this from the boat,' I said. 'No one gets in the water.'

Even from the boat the risks were extremely high.

There were pots all over the animal, around 20 in total, so we were going to have to really move around. We really didn't want to spend too much time positioned between a gigantic whale and a 32-tonne boat either. We were going to have to dart in, do the dirty work of cutting the lines and get back out again. I was also very conscious that we didn't want to injure the whale.

With a plan in place, we got to work. As the crew on Salcombe's lifeboat hoisted the first pot up, Chris and the diver were positioned on our bow with a sharp, hook-shaped knife at the ready. I drove us towards the other boat, but even that wasn't a simple task. The whale was clearly nervous and spooked by the activity going on around it. As I moved forward, it started to thrash and writhe around.

We had a powerful engine, but ultimately we were still just an inflatable boat sitting on a carpet of air, so as the whale moved we bounced around like a toy in a bath. Keeping steady, I realised I had a dilemma. If I needed to react quickly, say to reverse out of a dangerous position, I'd need to lock the engine down. But we had propellors.

I didn't want to be going astern and in doing so put a three-blade scar down the back of the whale.

If I was to keep everyone safe, including the whale, the job required complete focus. We moved in carefully and Chris took aim at the first line as the diver helped keep it in place. With a few deft flicks of the knife, the line parted and the crew on the all-weather lifeboat hauled the pot on deck, as I moved the D class away from the boat again to regroup.

One down, 19 to go.

Perhaps sensing some give, the whale began to move and came up again, making another high-pitched whine that sounded almost like a sorry little scream. This time we were a lot closer to its blowhole when it gasped for breath. As it did, it felt like our nostrils were under attack.

'Oooooof!' I said.

The smell …

We'd never smelled a whale's breath before, nor ever imagined what it might be like. But now we knew.

It smelled like a fish market.

It wasn't a disgusting rotting-fish smell. Just an extremely intense, warm aroma of fish and salty ocean. Being so close, it was almost overpowering, but its intensity faded as we moved away. It was quite an incredible moment, but we had no time to discuss it. That would have to be one for later. After all, if this didn't have a happy ending, no one would want to talk about it.

If we wanted that happy ending, we still had a lot more pots to cut away.

'There's one,' shouted one of the crew from Salcombe's boat.

I followed the direction of their finger pointing to our next target pot and we went again. Once it was off, the pot was hoisted up and the whale lurched again, this time moving the all-weather boat with it. The power of the whale was incredible. In exercises the ILB could pull the bigger boat, but it was a challenge – here the whale was doing it with ease. Its strength was amazing and really quite frightening.

Refocusing on the task at hand, we moved back and got into position for the next pot. For the first few goes, the whale fought every time it felt a line go. Salcombe's boat would be pointing east one minute, then down to the west the next.

They were really being pulled around.

But after a while, the whale's reactions became more muted. It stopped thrashing around and just became very, very still. Maybe it was just so exhausted that it had lost its fight, that it

222

was giving up. It was already astonishing that it could have survived the week with all this gear on it.

But then I thought:

Maybe it knows we're here to help.

Maybe it's helping us do our job by keeping still.

It seemed as plausible as anything else.

One by one we cut the lines, working as quickly as possible. The last thing we wanted was for the lines between whale and boat to part and for her to swim off still all tangled up in ropes and pots. If it did, the chances were that this time, it would drown, either weighed down by what it was carrying now or after being caught up in other gear out at sea. Everyone involved in the rescue pushed hard and we got into a rhythm.

Drive in.

Cut the line.

Hoist the pot.

Drive out.

Over and over, until there was just one pot left.

We'd been cutting the lines attached to each pot for almost an hour when I manoeuvred alongside again. By this point the physical exertion of hacking through each one meant Chris was exhausted. With the concentration needed to keep the boat steady and the propellor blades away from the whale, I was pretty mentally exhausted too.

We were almost there, but it still felt like such a way to go.

I took a deep breath and focused hard on keeping the boat in position.

'Not long now, mate,' I said.

I wasn't sure if it was for my benefit, Chris's or the whale's, but it had been a long slog and I imagined the team on Salcombe's boat felt the same too. I watched as Chris swiped the knife at the line again and again.

'It's not going easy,' he called to me.

'Keep at it,' I said. 'It's going.'

Sure enough, the line was starting to fray, but it just wasn't quite budging. The longer it took, the more likely I knew it was that the whale would move and we'd end up having to come round and have another go.

I watched, ready to make the move backwards if needed.

Come on, Chris, you've almost got it, I willed him on silently.

Swipe. Swipe. Swipe.

It was probably only a few minutes but it felt like an eternity.

And then, finally, *Whoooosh!*

'Yes!' Chris shouted. 'It's off!'

The crew on the all-weather boat swung into action, working together to get the pot up and onto the boat. As it landed with a hollow *thunk* on the deck, there were cheers up there too.

We'd done it!

Suddenly, the whale disappeared below the surface. I'd expected it to do just that, but as it did, I couldn't help thinking, had we been too late?

It might have had it.

But then the sea started shifting, waves rippling at the surface.

It was on the move.

The poor thing probably just wanted to head off and recover from its ordeal, stay underwater and away from ropes, pots, boats and noisy people.

At least it's OK, I thought.

'Dart to Salcombe. Good job there. We're heading back to the station,' we said over the radio. I honestly thought that was the last we'd see of the whale, until a couple of minutes later, just as we'd started to head back to the lifeboat station.

'Look!' shouted one of the crew, pointing ahead in the water.

'Ahh, there it is,' I said.

We could see the whale off to the boat's starboard side. It was just above the surface again, heading west across Start Bay.

It must have just needed a few minutes to compose itself. Now it was swimming powerfully along, not a single line or pot attached to it, cutting the waves with power and a grace that defied its enormous size.

Exactly as it should be.

I maneuvered the D-Class parallel to the whale, giving it plenty of space and pacing alongside. Looking over my shoulder, I spotted Salcombe's all-weather boat doing the same. With all the pots strewn across its deck, it looked more like a fishing vessel than a lifeboat.

After the high drama of the day, it was a beautiful, serene moment, in the early evening with the sun going down. Start Bay was peaceful and the pink-tinged sky made it look just like a picture postcard.

And here we were, powering alongside this awesome, awesome creature.

I didn't think a shout could end in a more magical way.

Then the whale ducked under the waves. For a moment it was gone, but soon a huge air bubble appeared on the surface of the water.

'It's coming up!' someone shouted.

Sure enough, the whale's head burst through the surface of the water, spraying a blast of air out of its blowhole, then almost its whole body leapt out of the sea, before crashing down.

We were all a bit overwhelmed by the emotion of what we'd just witnessed, not to mention the role each of us had played in saving this ocean giant. It was the kind of moment you only usually saw on wildlife programmes or in films. We all knew this was a once-in-a-lifetime moment, so just soaked it all in.

As it leapt up a second time, a lump caught in my throat.

As the whale sprayed fishy breath from its blowhole once more, it made a sound that was completely different to the eerie and pained cries we'd heard all day. It didn't sound weak or afraid. It was something else altogether.

If a whale could sound happy, that's exactly what I heard.

It was almost like it was saying thank you.

Showing us that it was fine.

As it crashed down a second time, it splashed its huge, spectacular tail against the water of Start Bay one last time, then disappeared into the distance, easily pulling away from our powerful boats.

As incredible as the experience had been, I never wanted a reason to see such a magnificent creature in that kind of distress again. When it was spotted in the bay three days later, happily swimming around, I was filled with pride knowing our two RNLI crews and the divers had made that possible.

Everything about the job was incredibly memorable. Working so closely with our flank station at Salcombe was a real bonding experience for the crews, and we all still reminisce about it. I'm 14 years with the lifeboat now and getting a bit long in the tooth compared with some of the others. I'd like to think that I'll get to my 20 years with the RNLI, but we'll see. It's almost four years since that shout now, and the moment the whale breached in front of us still sticks with me. I think it always will.

A WHISTLE-STOP TOUR OF THE RNLI'S COASTAL CANINE CREW

The furry, feathered and four-legged creatures that RNLI crew bravely save from the waves aren't the only creatures that form part of the charity's fabric and family. At lifeboat stations across the country, paws-on pets can be found playing their part in the RNLI's mission to save lives at sea.

Just like Cromer's famous Monte Blogg – faithful friend to the RNLI's most decorated lifeboat crew member, Henry Blogg – lifeboat station dogs are there to greet visitors, welcome volunteers back from long shouts and boost fund-raising efforts by deploying their most powerful skills – charm and cuteness.

The value of the RNLI's canine crew really cannot be over-estimated, and no book about the service that the RNLI provides to animals in distress would be complete without recognising the animals that do service to our crews and the communities they protect by providing care and companion-ship to all.

There are hundreds of lifeboat dogs in active service today, so these are just some of our four-legged favourites that you might meet on a whistle-stop tour round our coast.

At stations around north-east Scotland, including RNLI Dunbar, you'll find 18-month-old Goose, a Hungarian Vizsla who keeps watch over crew and lifeboats alike. Owned by RNLI area lifesaving manager Henry Weaver, Goose is a young pup following in some big pawprints. He joined the RNLI's canine crew last year after Archie, Henry's previous 'wingdog', sadly passed away. Henry says Goose still has a way to go to fill Archie's boots, but he's eager – and learning fast!

Travel 140 miles up the coast from Dunbar to Aberdeen Lifeboat Station and you might be lucky enough to meet not one but three 'morale officers': five-year-old Betty and her daughter, four-month-old Mish, both Belgian Malinois, and Gigha, a ten-year-old Belgian Malinois-German Shepherd cross. Owned by coxswain/mechanic Cal Reed and his partner Jenny, the trio greet crew and visitors with equal enthusiasm, meaning the station is never short of friendly faces. When they're not curled under Cal's desk (leaving little room for his feet), they can be found keeping guests company on the sofa or watching the lifeboat coming back from a shout. Gigha, Betty and Mish all pick up the mantle from Cal's previous station dog Monte – named after Henry Blogg's dog – who was a well-loved character around the harbour. Monte sadly passed away in 2019, but Cal says that he thinks he would be very impressed by the new station dogs' excellent work!

On Scotland's west coast, Tobermory Lifeboat Station's pampered pooch Diesel is described by his crewmates as an 'RNLI supermodel'. The svelte seven-year-old Springer Spaniel originates from the Scottish Borders and has a few field trial champions in his line. He grew up at the station after former coxswain Andrew McHaffie got him as a puppy. When Andrew became fleet staff coxswain, his role took him away from home so lifeboat operations manager and former crew member and navigator Sam Jones took Diesel in. Happiest surrounded by people who will shower him with attention, Diesel's favourite game is ball search and rescue – or 'BallSAR'. 'He loves to search for his tennis balls when out walking,' says Sam. 'He does real search patterns, which probably not only reflects his breed, but also the time he spends around the station and the crew.' Sam also manages community projects for the RNLI, so when he is away, crew member Leanne Blair looks after Diesel. Moving down the coast and over the border into Cumbria, you'll find a growing family of station dogs at Silloth RNLI, including Roxy, the chocolate Lab. When her owner Andrew Stanley fulfilled his lifelong dream to join the crew, Roxy wasn't far behind, and she soon became a friendly and familiar face at the station, boosting morale with her good nature. As well as guarding the station's lifeboat, Roxy now also has a trainee lifeboat dog in her care – Elsie, Andrew's fox-red Labrador. Roxy works hard to keep her in check and teaches her all she knows!

South-west of Silloth, out in the Irish Sea, the Isle of Man has a mischievous member of canine crew. Stationed at RNLI Douglas, Dhoona – or 'Dark Maiden' in Manx – is a one-year-old Bearded Collie who could be considered head of visitor experience on account of her friendly nature. She likes to lend a paw when stowing the tow line but, less helpfully, she also enjoys stealing the station loo roll (usually while you're on the loo, her dad, mechanic Tony Radcliffe, tells us). When she's bored, she loves nothing more than removing the crew's socks from their wellies, one by one.

Over in Ireland there's no shortage of dedicated furry volunteers either. Bosco the Parson Jack Russell dons his special RNLI coat to greet visitors and 'lead' school and youth group visits at Carrybridge Lifeboat Station. Taught well by his owner, crew member Jen Bailey and her father, lifeboat operations manager Tom Bailey, Bosco's favourite thing in life is playing fetch with his tennis balls, but food and lifeboats come a very close second.

At Dun Laoghaire RNLI you'll find Jed, a three-year-old Terrier mix with a winning character and a knack for finding lost balls. Since being adopted from Wicklow SPCA by mechanic Kieran O'Connell, Jed has visited the station every morning. He's always on hand to meet and greet crew and visitors – when he's not sleeping, that is! According to Kieran, Jed's favourite spot for a dognap is in the office in-tray, which catches the best of the morning sunshine.

Over on England's north-west coast, ten-year-old Golden Retriever Bob – or 'Boathouse Bobby', as he's lovingly known – is a regular fixture at New Brighton Lifeboat Station. Always in attendance alongside his owner, lifeboat operations manager Ian Thornton, Bob's duties include being cute and entertaining visiting members of the public. When he's not hard at work, Bob's favorite pastime is scrounging treats – and he's very good at that!

Travel south down the coast to Cornwall and eventually you'll reach Sennen Cove RNLI. If you're lucky you might just see Piran, a six-year-old Collie, in the lifeboat station shop, alongside his best pal and former crew member Steven Phillips. Named after St Piran, the patron saint of miners, because he was bought at a pig farm on the saint's day (5 March), Steve has clear memories of meeting his companion. 'I got him in a rush as he was the last dog left. He was covered from head to toe in manure when I put him in the back seat of the car and he got pig muck everywhere. Cost me a fortune to valet!'

Steven served as lifeboat crew in Penlee from 1979, before moving to The Lizard in late 1980. He started volunteering in the shop at Sennen Cove in 2020. When he increased his hours he started bringing Piran to work too, and he's proved to be a natural in the retail game. Now the official 'head of welcoming', Piran makes sure customers get a warm reception and he loves the attention he receives in return. Piran also enjoys running on the beach before heading into the shop to work, as well as the occasional pint with Steven at their local pub, The Kings Arms in St Just.

If you spot Cowes lifeboat operations manager Mark Southwell on the Isle of Wight in the south-east of England, he'll almost certainly be flanked by one of two Collie-Labrador-cross pooches. Mickey, Cowes RNLI's longest-serving lifeboat dog, has retired from duty in recent years, handing over as head of station security to his young protégé Maisie. As well as their dedicated service, Mark also fondly recalls a moment walking the pair in the park when his pager sounded. As he jogged to the station with the dogs in tow, Mickey decided he needed to do his business – well, when you've got to go, you've got to go! Mark swiftly scooped up after him and continued to the station, arriving with a full poo bag swinging in one hand – 'It's not all romantic heroics at the RNLI!' he said.

While Mickey and Maisie might be two of Cowes' most recognisable pooches, they're certainly not the only ones. In fact, nearly half of the station crew – 20 people out of 50 – have 24 dogs between them. On any given day you could bump into Molly, Tilley, Winnie, Raven, Finn, Hugo, Daisy, Luna, Hobart, Marley, Frank, Maggie, Rosie, Captain, Max, Meg, Molly, Panther, Peppi, Mabel, Prim, Katie or Mabel.

A veritable haven for hounds, the location of the slipway at Cowes also means that dogs' toy balls lost in the Solent regularly get washed up among the seaweed. With such an extensive canine crew to entertain, the team 'recycles' the balls by keeping them on the window ledge in the boat hall ready to use – until the dogs lose them again, that is!

At Dungeness RNLI, Border Collie-Poodle cross Woolly shares the same rugged good looks as his owner, operations manager and second mechanic Roger Gillett. At least that's what Roger tells us! Once the star of an RNLI Christmas card, Woolly's *real* duties include entertaining children visiting the station, guarding the launch and recovery equipment for the station's Shannon-class lifeboat, assisting with crew training and doing the odd spot of admin.

Finally, in the seaside town of Aldeburgh in Suffolk, Labrador and lifelong lifeboat dog George is a well-loved member of the local community – even more popular than the station itself, according to crew! Always at the side of his owner, coxswain Steve Saint, George accompanies him to Aldeburgh

Lifeboat Station every day. George gives visitors to the station a very warm welcome (usually in pursuit of a biscuit), and helps with crew health-and-safety briefings. If he looks like he's lazing on the beach, don't be fooled – he's secretly guarding the lifeboat in the boathouse!

To these and all of our beloved 'paw-some' lifeboat dogs – of past, present and future crew – thank you for your service!

ACKNOWLEDGEMENTS

This book would not have been possible without the dedication, skill and kind co-operation of the following people: James Anthony, Nardia Bissmire, Luke Blissett, Mark Bolland, Scott Brierley, Lucy Brown, Amy Caldwell, Mike Carhart-Harris, Becky Cheers, Clare Cocks, Mel Cooper, Alan Cracknell, Nikki Croft-Girvan, Alice Dewsnap, Steve Doherty, Hattie Evans, Ian Farrall, Lydia Good, Sim Greenaway, Sarah Hammond, Oliver Harvey, Rowena and Tim Heale, Myles Hussey, Terry Jeacock, Phil John, Ashley Jones, Emily Jones, Vince Jones, John McCarter, Jamie Mathys, Morgan Meaker, Pete Murphy, Isobel Noctor, Harriet Prideaux, Mark Pusey, Jim Rice, Kevin Smith, Rory Stamp, Ed Thomas, Hayley Whiting, Nathan Williams, Chris Winzar and Ollie Wrynne-Simpson.

PICTURE CREDITS

Page 1, top: RNLI
Page 1, bottom: RNLI/Vince Jones
Page 2, top: RNLI/Mel Cooper
Page 2, bottom: RNLI/David Clarke
Page 3: RNLI
Page 4, top: RNLI/Chris Green
Page 4, bottom: Gareth Davies
Page 5, top: Row Heale
Page 5, bottom: RNLI/Joe Joyce
Page 6: RNLI
Page 7, inset: RNLI/Ed Thomas
Page 7, main: RNLI/Jordan Summersgill
Page 8, top: RNLI/Cowes
Page 8, bottom: RNLI/Riki Bannister

Lifeboats

Get closer to the lifesavers

For more stories from the RNLI's lifesavers, visit:
RNLI.org/magazine

Follow the RNLI on Facebook, Twitter and Instagram
for the charity's latest rescues, updates and fascinating history:
Facebook.com/RNLI | Twitter.com/RNLI | Instagram.com/RNLI

Thank you for powering the charity that saves lives at sea

A GIFT IN YOUR WILL
IS OUR PROTECTION AT SEA

To find out how you can create a lifesaving legacy,
visit RNLI.org/waves

6 in 10
LAUNCHES
ARE ONLY POSSIBLE THANKS TO
GIFTS IN WILLS

RNLI Lifeboats

DOG OWNERS:

DON'T PADDLE AFTER YOUR DOG!

'Sooooo excited! When I get in I'm gonna swim and swim and …'

Toby (2)
Full-time Border Collie

YOU'RE **TOP DOG** DON'T RISK YOUR LIFE

If your dog swims out too far, do not go after them! Move to a place they can get to safely and call them. Most will get back by themselves.

RNLI.org/TopDog

IF YOU'RE WORRIED **CALL 999** AND ASK FOR THE **COASTGUARD**

#RESPECT THE WATER